How to Survive and Thrive in an Impossible World

Steve Carter / Steve Bonham

How to Survive and Thrive in an Impossible World

Steve Carter / Steve Bonham

Copyright © 2025 Steve Carter / Steve Bonham.
All rights reserved.

Design by Christopher Lydon.
Illustrations by Dewayne Ashton.

No part of this book can be reproduced in any form,
by written, electronic or mechanical, including photocopying,
recording, or by any information retrieval system
without written permission from the author.

Published by Artisan Creative Ltd, Derbyshire, UK.
artisan-creative.com

Although every precaution has been taken in the preparation of this book, the publisher and author assume no responsibility for errors or omissions. Neither is any liability assumed for damages resulting from the use of information contained herein.

ISBN (paperback) 978-1-7384035-3-0
ISBN (e-book) 978-1-7384035-4-7

Contents

Introduction to the second edition 5
Preface: Haunted by Guitars 9
Part One: The State We're In 19
    Chapter 1: This Precarious Life 21
    Chapter 2: The Fear of Fear 31
    Chapter 3: How We Got Here 43
    Chapter 4: The Story So Far 55
Part Two: Solid Ground 67
    Chapter 5: Natural Resilience 69
    Chapter 6: The Possibility of You 79
    Chapter 7: The Captain of Your Ship 99
    Chapter 8: The Rewilded Self 117
Part Three: Five Practices for a Wholehearted Life 133
    Chapter 9: Readiness 135
    Chapter 10: Be Wild 143
    Chapter 11: Be Strong 161
    Chapter 12: Be Experimental 181
    Chapter 13: Travel With Companions 199
    Chapter 14: Take the First Step 221
Thanks 239
About the author 243

Introduction to the second edition

Since the first edition was published five years ago, this book has taken on a life of its own.

It's been turned into an 'interactive, wellbeing, musical show thingy' and enjoyed a three-week run at Edinburgh Festival Fringe and a run at Brighton Fringe. The show has been performed for frontline NHS staff and across England as a Rural Touring event.

An EP of the songs inspired by the book has been recorded and received global airplay.

As a talk, with or without music, it has been featured at Wigtown Book Festival, numerous U3A (University of the Third Age) events, and other events across the country.

Through all of this, the magnificent Chris 'the Bishop' Lydon has been co-presenter, musical director, creative producer, book designer and ringmaster to the madness. I cannot thank him enough, and remain utterly in awe of his ability to *sort things out*.

It was through the intensity and exuberance of the performances – and the conversations that followed – that the original ideas behind the book were strengthened and developed, until it became vital to capture and include them. Thank you to all those who came and lingered to talk afterwards.

This second edition is not so much a revision of the first, but a regeneration! Ideas implicit in the first suddenly burst into life and demanded attention. The link with rewilding was a pure example of serendipity, inspired by reading George Monbiot's book *Feral*, Isabella Tree's marvellous *Wilding*, and Chantal Lyons' *Groundbreakers*; filtered through a dozen walks and watching the seas slide by on a sailing holiday.

Many thanks to Jonathan Males, William Winstone and Sheenah Jones, whose wisdom and careful reading of key chapters has been massively helpful.

As with the first time around, my old friend Peter Harvey has brought his amazing proofing skills to this manuscript, impossible deadlines met with ease. Any mistakes that remain herein are most definitely mine.

Finally, thanks and love to Orla, for whom I have been a distracted partner for many months, and whose conviction in the worth of this book both inspired me to write and rewrite it.

Steve Carter / Steve Bonham
Doveridge, Derbyshire, England
May 2025

Steve Bonham is a 'nom de plume' for my creative works and Steve Carter is my name, both personally and professionally, as a psychologist and consultant. Most of the time I am one and the same!

Preface: Haunted by Guitars

I was 16 and quite bright – well, not dumb anyway. No sporting prowess to speak of. Largely ignored by the opposite sex. I guess a bit of an outsider. I used to play the trumpet but had given up because of the floppy lips and a distinct lack of cool. At school I did okay, in a rather erratic sort of way. My school reports were all along the lines of, 'Capable, but unpredictable.' I had no real idea of where my life was going or what I wanted to do. My own vague idea was that I might be a Spitfire pilot, except the war was over and, anyway, I was short-sighted.

Mr Hertzberg, our careers master, suggested to me, 'Have you considered being a town and country planner?' I hadn't and still haven't.

And then one afternoon, I went to see some friends who were in a band and were rehearsing for a little gig they had that evening. I'd not taken much notice of what they had been doing until that point, but they were good friends and I had a vague interest in music. I arrived at the venue. There was Keith on bass, looking slightly confused, and Kev on drums, and Foss and Paul with guitars. These two were sitting on the edge of the stage. And as I came through the door, they started to play this rather lovely instrumental. When they finished, I asked, 'What's that? I've never heard it before.' Paul looked at me and said, 'Well, it's one of ours. We just wrote it.' 'Oh,' I said, 'What's it called?' 'Instrumental Number Two. It not being the first.'

I was astonished. It was the first time I had been made aware that ordinary folks like us could write songs. I thought it was a specialist job undertaken by people who knew lots of theory and lots of arcane rules. Not written by my friends. Or by me.

It was as if I had been simultaneously struck by a bolt of lightning, a roar of thunder, and a few other hallelujahs from an angelic host. The path of my life was now as clear as it ever would be. That's what I must do. I must play guitar in a band and I must write lovely tunes, like Instrumental Number Two. It was undeniable, incontrovertible, and completely unavoidable.

But then I went to university and, three years later, as I sat on the edge of my life, looking at my guitar and looking at my degree, I hesitated and went down the road of becoming a psychologist.

But that guitar never ever stopped haunting me, calling me, and reproaching me for the life I might have lived. However, my adventures in psychology, usually working with organisations all over the world as a consultant in leadership performance, have taught me this: we all have a virtual guitar we put away to join this strange thing called 'the real world.' We have surrendered, buried, ignored, forgotten, sold and belittled aspects of who we are so that we can join in and survive. It's a fatal compromise. We are born with so much more than we become. We are abundant with possibility. This is a book about liberation, and we do need to liberate ourselves to cope, to survive and still to thrive. We live in weird times.

I love the word 'weird.' It comes from the Anglo-Saxon. It means 'unknowable.' Disturbing, as if some strange gods are playing with our destiny that we don't understand. A kind of strange fate. Most things we know and understand are under siege. How do we live a life that works for us in weird times? How do we get a sense of agency in our lives? I believe we need to radically reorient ourselves in our relationship with the world.

There was an old deal between us ordinary folk and the world. It demanded from us a 'servant mindset' and it was a way of having some sort of life. It was based upon a simple process, mindless enough to make it scalable. This was: if you fit in and do what is expected of you and accept being told who you are, in return you will be offered survival, protection and some sort of comfort. It was – as we shall see – the price of belonging to a tribe. At first, this was an agreement between equals. A common theme amongst the original peoples in all the places in which I have rambled has been a near lack of status. This seems to have been true amongst the Berbers, the San Bushmen, Cherokee and the Cree: leadership was something given by the tribe to one or more people and something that could be taken away. Wherever possible, major decisions seemed to have involved the whole community.

However, as societies grew more complex, institutions and individuals made power grabs and the idea of master and servant grew. Quickly, the deal stopped being between equal parties; but it still worked for enough people to make it viable.

But now it seems that the deal is broken.

If you are expecting a career, you won't have one. And marriage, you won't stay in one. A place to live, you'll move frequently. A salary, you won't get one. A mortgage, you can't afford it. Fitter, you'll be fatter. Retirement? Really?

We live in a time of the random, the stupid and arbitrary. A weird world that carries no assurance, whose defining characteristic is uncertainty. And the things that would have looked after us in the past are crumbling. So, the offer 'work hard and you will have the money to survive' doesn't really do it in these times. So how do we really survive and thrive in the weird normal?

That is what I want to explore with you. This book is not just a survival book; it's a 'thrival' book. I want to explore with you not just how to 'get by', but how to rescue the artisan, the explorer, the magician and even the guitar player within!

Some might say I'm not a good example. If this book claimed it was about making you rich and successful, then I would be a fraud. I am not rich, but I'm not poor. I have a nice house, but it's not a mansion. My car is second-hand. My health is distinctly average. I am fit enough but could lose a few pounds.

But then people sometimes tell me, 'Hey, you're living the dream.' What do they mean? Well, I am a musician now, some of the time. I've released several albums. I've written books. I've travelled the world over and met some extraordinary people. I have slept in some of the finest hotels, and out on the ground in the Sahara Desert bewitched by the stars. I believe that I have helped other people dream again and achieve good things. It is rare that I don't, when I'm at home, sit at my desk in the morning, looking out at the oak tree standing outside my window and feeling optimistic and encouraged. I feel, in an almost mysterious way, liberated.

These learnings have been hard won. I've known dark times, as we all do. I have been treated for depression. I have been nearly bankrupt. I have faced catastrophe. So, the things that helped me pull through and which I've used to help others are the things I'd like to share with you. For I believe that for nearly all of us, a reassessment is due in our relationship with the world. For what we expect will not be delivered. These days, I think of myself as a field psychologist. And, just as often, a vagabond philosopher. A field psychologist, because although I am well qualified in this profession, I am someone whose learning is augmented and enriched and given practical insight by a deep engagement with the world. And a vagabond philosopher, because in 30 years of travel in every continent, the ongoing conversations with people and places has challenged me to think about who I am, who we are, and how we can lead a more fulfilling life.

So, what am I offering? Not really a step-by-step route map, a quick fix, but a best chance to liberate your 'wholeself' and more closely follow the life you want to live. To change your relationship with yourself and the world.

And how do you do this? Take a trip down the shelves of a bookstore, real or virtual, and there will be row upon row of books aimed at helping you improve your life: how to succeed, how to lose weight, how to be more attractive, how to be more intelligent, how to, how to, how to. My favourite is how to roll a joint. I think it was a joke! The trouble is most of them don't work. If one of them did, in almost any category, the market for that sort of book would collapse. The thing most have in common is they ask you to set goals and regularly monitor how you are doing. This is the heart of so many aspects of our lives at the moment: we are all given targets, goals, and objectives and are mercilessly measured against them at school, in sport, in work, in our lives.

They are so persuasive, and pervasive. And it's not just enough to have one goal; we are given many, often in competition with each other; sub-goals, short-term goals, medium-term goals, long-term goals, milestones – or is it millstones? And they don't work. Goals cannot be the primary mechanism for personal change in liberation because firstly, they psychologically miss the point, and secondly, they are desperately impractical. Plus, they are based upon assumptions of how the world works which are quite frankly barmy. Goals are something you can develop *after* you have read this book!

My first law of change is: *open yourself up to what is on offer!*

So often in my professional life, I have seen the look of almost panic on someone's face when they have been asked: 'What do you want do with your life?' 'What's your ultimate goal?!' 'What's your vision for yourself?' You can't know this until you know the possibility of who you are and understand deeply and how you might engage in different ways with the world.

When I look back at that moment in time when I saw what I wanted to do and did something else, it wasn't a lack goals that led me astray, but a lack of readiness, a false understanding of what the world offered, and a broken understanding of my relationship with it. In a nutshell, I'd failed to see what the world, or rather the society I was born into, was doing and had not realised it had taken me hostage.

Liberation is about bringing all the aspects of who we are into our relationship with the world. It is, as we shall see, the process of revising, recovering, and regenerating our strengths, the things we are good at and passionate about.

For years I teased away at this problem: why we so often do what we nearly want to do, rather than what we really want to do? I explored it in my book *A Little Nostalgia for Freedom*, some of the stories from which I include here.

It was at that moment that I saw the importance of standing strong and ready. Adaptable, where searching is the key for a better life. It all boils down to this: flourishing in these weird times is not achieved through the single-minded pursuit of goals, but through crafting an approach to life that is built upon your strengths, your inspiration, your authenticity, and your hands-on experience of living in the world.

So, if you feel like your career is stuck, that things don't add up, or you've got that haunting feeling, 'Is this it?' then this book is for you. Or perhaps you're feeling overwhelmed, beaten down by the absurdity of it all. If you feel a bit adrift or just totally confused over what to do next, this book is for you.

This book is organised into three parts.

Part One explores 'the state we're in' – how evolution and socialisation might be shaping us to be less than we might be and how that impacts us in terms of how we deal with uncertainty and risk. How we can come to understand how the story we tell about ourselves reflects and reinforces this.

Part Two focuses on our 'solid ground' – what will be the building blocks of change towards a more liberated, abundant life. This will include rediscovering our natural resilience and the innate possibility of ourselves. It covers the need to create mental headspace for change by taking a more stoical stance on life and moving through the mindful gap, mischief zone and the creative space. And finally, it invites you to rewild yourself to liberate your 'wholeself' to live a more abundant life.

Part Three offers five 'practices' to develop your practical agency. These five practices, or 'rules of the road', build the solid ground to survive and thrive in this Impossible World.

Look, I know this is a 'how to' book, but it isn't a prescription. What I would like to do is share with you some of my journey, literally and figuratively, and introduce you to what I have learned along the road. And I really believe – in fact, it is a theme of this book! – that we can learn from everywhere and apply it anywhere.

And I don't know whether you picked up this book to explore changes in your working life or your personal life, but I should confess straightaway I don't see the difference. The idea of work-life balance was always a bizarre concept which seemed to see life split into two discrete elements. Your life contains your work and you work better when you bring your whole life to it. This takes craftsmanship, and it requires a liberated mindset. It promises a more joyful and purposeful story.

From my stories and ideas, my hope is that you can fashion a life that works for you. A wholehearted life.

Part One:
The State We're In

Chapter 1: This Precarious Life

Is life getting impossible?

We live in weird times. Oligarchs and plastic princes strut across the world stage, despots glisten in their tin pot glory, respect is replaced with derision. The weak are mocked and the strong belittled. Boundaries are betrayed. Right or left demand blind loyalty and spotlight their hatred on non-believers.

The Enlightenment – the idea that evidence and reason should guide our decisions and actions – is undone. The world seems disenchanted with itself – out of control, even disintegrating.

Weird.

Weird is the Saxon word for unknowable. Unpredictable and uncertain.

Too many people feel they are living life like polar bears on the melting ice, or hedgehogs crossing the path of the road roller of destiny.

I am writing these words as the media is full of danger and threat. The consensus about how we all can coexist on this planet and the institutions that have been built to sustain that consensus have been trashed. The old certainties have been ruptured. 'Things fall apart; the centre cannot hold.' Meanwhile, the world ominously warms.

I guess nearly all of us feel now and then that life is, well, a little precarious. For many, including people you will most definitely know, it feels horribly threatening as if they are walking a very narrow wall, worried that any moment they could fall off. For others there is a deep feeling of being trapped, not able to express properly who they are or who they want to be.

The world in short feels impossible.

How do you respond to this Impossible World and all the reasons to despair within it? The temptations to hide are many. The temptations to blame are more. And in doing so we know we make the whole thing worse. Perhaps it's not surprising that people feel increasingly powerless. That globally rates of mental distress soar.

And it might not just be the specific horrors of these times but an insidious, underlying process of disempowerment. It might seem a bit radical, but you could argue that the process of becoming an adult is, at least in part, a process of learning to be helpless, endlessly discovering our vulnerability and our powerlessness. We discover that there are others with inconceivable amounts of power, and we recognise their blindness to our needs. We learn the limitations to our decision making and our autonomy, as the often-unseen forces that shape who we are demand our dependability and compliance.

In the 1960s the eminent psychologist Martin Seligman developed the concept of learned helplessness. In a series of experiments with his colleague Steven F Maier, he showed how individuals, faced with uncontrollable negative events can rapidly become demotivated, anxious, and depressed with little energy in the pursuit of what they want and need. After some time, this learned helplessness becomes ongoing and persistent.

In short, it is a reaction to our perception of the world as being malign and uncontrollable, and that there is nothing we can do about it.

And this is a state of mind that continues even when the means to control and influence what is going on becomes available or demonstrated.

My contention is that in the face of seemingly greater and greater evidence of the chaos, the arbitrariness, and the malignancy of the world, driven through the poisonous swamp of social media, people are at the same time losing their capacity to deal with it. The chaos is getting, if not worse, at least more visible and, psychologically, our ability to cope with it is weakening.

Are we witnessing a global epidemic of learned helplessness? People are beginning to define their identity by their fears and phobias, and politicians are lining up to lever this helplessness.

Populist politicians state over and over again 'you are broken, we need to be made great again, I am the one to do it.'

More liberal politicians say 'I feel your pain, but we can change the world so the pain goes away. We can protect you; we will care for you if you just leave it with us.'

Both messages are the same. What neither wonders is how can 'I' help you help yourself. No one questions whether you should feel helpless. In fact, many politicians go out of their way to make you feel worse, painting scenarios of doom and disaster, threat, and trauma. For your helplessness is the hook by which they ensnare you.

At the heart of our anxiety, chronic or specific, our frustrations with the world, is the wriggling little mental worm 'nothing I can do can change things.' Big things like global warming, pandemics, war, and the cost-of-living crisis. Smaller things like my job, my weight, my relationships, my mental and physical health.

That is a real danger as we hunker down in this madness, draw ourselves in, seek protection that we become less than we might be. We surrender the possibility of an abundant life.

I don't want the argument to sound dismissive, as if our struggles with the madness in this world are somehow our fault, and that we should simply pull up our britches and get over it. The dramatic increases in mental health problems like chronic anxiety, depression and phobias are real enough. That society and its leaders need to step up and tackle the causes of them is unarguable. But alongside that, surely, there is a part to be played by ourselves.

This is a book for those of you who feel life can be a struggle to control your world, to feel you are standing on solid ground, who want to feel liberated from a sense of being pushed and buffeted by uncaring forces. It's for those who feel they must shrink themselves to survive, give up some of that which they believe. For those who define themselves by their anxieties, fears, and phobias. But the title of the book implies that life is not just about surviving; it is as much about thriving. And to thrive you need to open yourself to the possibility of yourself. For none of us starts with nothing; we stand on the shoulders of all the evolutionary and cultural gifts our ancestors have bestowed upon us. And as my dear late friend Philip Lindsay used to remark 'all our weaknesses are but wrongly played strengths.'

This is a book about rediscovering our natural resilience by building what I would like to call 'practical agency.' Practical agency is about how you understand and use your ability to shape your life experience. Do you feel enabled to act independently, to solve problems, meet challenges, to greet this Impossible World head on? Do you feel the fears and anxieties you face are something that you can overcome in order to embrace a fuller, richer experience of life? Or do you feel you turn in on yourself, draw in your involvement, accept your anxieties and fears as part of who you are, your identity even?

Seeing the possibility within and without

At its heart lies a fundamental sense of who you are and how the world is. Do you see the possibility of yourself as limited or abundant?

For reasons I can no longer recall, many years ago I was quite taken with the ideas of José Ortega y Gasset, a Spanish philosopher who lived in exile from the fascist dictator Franco, in France and Argentina. He hated the drift to the bland and the mediocre, which would be the result for almost everyone if the extremes of either the left or the right dominated. Instead, he saw life as a creative act in which we all took part and were responsible for writing our own part.

'Our world is not an object to be grasped but a drama in which we must participate' and we are 'not a mere passenger in existence.'[1]

He writes about 'an abundance of possibility being a symptom of a thriving life.' But this abundance is not because we are born into riches or become super wealthy but is based upon a view of ourselves and our own individual existence.

To me, it's about having belief in your own potential, it is trusting in the possibility you hold within yourself. And relishing the creative act that mobilising that requires.

And the idea that we settle for less than we might be does seem a little sad. What's the point? Unless you have fully bought into self-conscious reincarnation this is the one life you've got, and you may as well make the most of it.

In an article in the British *Guardian* newspaper (19 April 2025), the Dutch historian and author Rutger Bregman asks the uncomfortable question: 'So what do you want on your resume? Do you want to go for a respectable but bland list? Or do you set the bar higher?'

He introduces the idea of 'moral ambition', the will to make the world a better place. 'Morally ambitious people don't move with the herd,' he writes, 'but believe in a deeper form of

---

[1] *Revolt of the Masses*, José Ortega y Gasset, W. W. Norton and Company, 1994 edition.

freedom. It's the freedom to push aside conventional standards of success, to make your own way along life's path, knowing it's a journey that you can only make once.'

The notion about finding your own way as a deeper form of freedom resonates deeply with me. Bregman reminds us that so many of us, not all certainly, have choices we can take about our careers, our contribution to the world, our willingness to confront the issues that face society and even the world. It is one of the most critical decisions we make in a whole series of life choices about the path we take through life or, as I shall describe it, the story we write about ourselves.

Moral ambition plays an essential but not complete part in what you might call a 'full life.' A full life is an abundant life when you set out to explore and experiment with all that you might be, engaging your 'wholeself.'

Your wholeself is the sum of all that you might be emotionally, intellectually, spiritually, and physically. To live *wholeheartedly* is to engage with this potential with an open heart. It is about embracing your vulnerability, your authenticity, accepting your faults and failures and moving on, shedding the masks you wear to be your true self without fear of judgement. It is to live with passionate intent.

A full life is not the same as aiming for some great achievement like wealth, fame, heroic status or even sainthood. Just the quiet determination to be the best person you can be with the gifts and opportunities you have been given. The possibility of us is endless. We can be parent, friend, competitor, rebel, carer, creator, artist, artisan, explorer, and experimenter and much else. And it is in the richness of this we could find the robust inner strength not just to cope with an Impossible World but learn to thrive in it.

And here's the thing: opening ourselves to the potential we hold, taking on a life which acknowledges that risks are there to be managed, may be a better way of coping than anything else.

This is a book about developing a new relationship with the world – a wholehearted one.

It's a book about unlearning our 'learned helplessness' and grasping the abundant potential we hold.

Chapter 2: The Fear of Fear

So, we live in times of massive uncertainty and chaos. And every day, our faces are rubbed in it with the 24/7 news and poisonous swamp of social media.

But was it ever thus? Ever since a herd of elephants crashed through a Neolithic village, flattening all before them, or a raging flood swept away the crops awaiting harvest, or an asteroid wiped out the dinosaurs, life has had its moments of mayhem. I remember once being on a track in the Namibian Bush when we had our dinner stolen on – I think – three separate occasions by other animals. A story as old as humankind.

The truth is we have never really lived in times of steadiness and tranquillity interrupted now and then by the odd explosion of madness, but rather in the buffeting torrent of unpredictability in which the occasional bubbles of sanity and security float.

Risk at any time is inevitable, safety an illusion.

How do we live a life that works for us in these times? How do we get a sense of agency in our lives? How do we make, if not friends with the fear that arises from this uncertainty, at least collaborative acquaintances?

In a world that feels increasingly uncertain, many of us have been raised to seek safety in certainty, to trust that someone else – an expert, an authority, an algorithm – has the right answer.

Does our education and upbringing result in us being encouraged to be risk-averse, to avoid failure at all costs, and to sidestep the discomfort of the unknown? From an early age, we are conditioned to value correctness over curiosity. Education systems reward standardised answers and penalise exploration, reinforcing the idea that problems have clear solutions rather than being complex, evolving challenges. Students learn to rely on prescribed formulas rather than developing the resilience to experiment, fail, and adapt. Or they increasingly seek to literally and metaphorically 'copy-and-paste' someone else's 'right answer'.

But what if the very challenges of an 'Impossible World' demand that we reclaim our ability to navigate uncertainty on our own terms? In this Impossible World, certainty is an illusion. No single authority has all the answers, and no risk-free path exists. If we are to truly survive and thrive, we must reclaim our ability to experiment, to sit with uncertainty, and to trust our own capacity for ingenuity. Rather than waiting for permission, for the 'right' answer, we must step forward and create our own. We must wholeheartedly seek out our 'wholeself'. And we must not be afraid to be afraid. This longing for a fear-free world is a teasing, dissembling mirage and through it we lose this resilience with which we can cope.

Where we once walked with beasts, we now hide among the daisies

All in all, it is probably a good idea not to find yourself surprised by the unexpected even if that is what a surprise is. Not being surprised by the unexpected is the first step in developing the ability to adapt and bounce back from the madness. It is about accepting risk into our lives in a way that is manageable and productive. It is acknowledging that being afraid is an unavoidable part of life. Dealing with fear is a life skill essential for our response to uncertainty and risk. Is it one we are losing?

Consider the proliferation of trigger warnings at the start of TV shows, films, and stage productions. While originally intended to offer consideration to those with past trauma, they have now extended to the most ordinary of human experiences: heartbreak, loss, tension, even excitement. It seems we are being conditioned to pre-emptively fear discomfort, as though being unsettled or uncertain is itself a kind of harm.

I am told that even Shakespeare plays now must have trigger warnings. What happened to the idea that you might take the trouble to find out the content of, say, King Lear before you go? Although Hamlet contains some jokes, the fact that it is labelled 'tragedy' might perhaps suggest taking some personal responsibility for a preliminary checking? This may seem a trivial example, but it suggests that managing risk and uncertainty is becoming a job to be outsourced to – hopefully – well-meaning others.

A good example of this cultural shift is with what Chantal Lyons calls, in her wonderful book *Groundbreakers* about the return of wild boar to the UK, 'Zoophobia'. She is struck by how afraid many people have learned to become of large animals. How we must be protected from them.

Zoophobia is the fear of beasts: in our zoologically impoverished island we seem unable to psychologically co-exist with other animals – particularly the bigger ones.

Groundbreakers explores the complexity of our relationship with wild boar which seem in mysterious ways to be reintroducing themselves into the UK. Something that alarms great numbers of people. But this fear is a specific example of a fear of anything 'wild'.

"We stripped out the aurochs, bear, boar, and wolf-species that could have harmed us in fury or self-defence even if they weren't our predators. After the loss of most big animals, we proceeded to steadily eliminate other wildlife from our lives. Already on an island, we made an island of ourselves.'

The result is a lack of knowledge and understanding of how to respond to the perceived threat of other animals when we find ourselves alongside them. Chantal Lyons goes onto highlight some bizarre examples in the media of this phobia.

'Vicious badger roams Scots school grounds as farmer warns parents' (Daily Record); *'Man calls 999 because he's scared of a hedgehog'* (ITN News); and *'Rewilding of Horsham Park a 'mad idea' amid fears long grass could house 'lots of insects'''* (Sussex Express).

There seems to be a growing fear of cattle. The press enjoys frequent stories of murderous attacks by the frenzied ruminators. But the truth is, it appears, more reassuring. In any one year if you take out accidents with farmhands and foolish people with uncontrolled off the lead dogs you are twice as likely to be killed by lightning than by a cow, and four times more likely to drown in a swimming pool.

Now the point is *not* that cattle are completely safe animals. Their size and herd instinct gives them the potential for harm.

This has always been the case. But our lack of experience and responsibility has left many people hanging by the field gate all avoiding the path altogether. Probably grumbling that the farmer has left the cattle in the field just to spoil the walk.

Where we once walked with beasts, we now hide among the daisies. Our ancestors would have understood the threat from other animals and respected and even celebrated it. But they knew that hiding amongst the daisies would mean that they would never do what they needed to do, never get where they needed to get. Never become who they want to be.

Looked at one way, an Impossible World is a wild world and risk a consequence of being in it.

Fear as a friend

And anyway, being afraid is not always a negative. Fear is a Swiss Army knife of a tool. It sharpens our thinking, summons our creativity, gives us focus, engages us, prepares us for action. Fear is a useful response to perceived risk. It makes the climber check their fixing of the ropes as they ascend the cliff face, the chef weigh their ingredients carefully.

It makes us resilient and experienced judges of the evolving threat in our world. If uncertainty creates risk, then fear is the battery that drives our ability to respond to it. Of course, overwhelming risk creates panic, blind avoidance, or even total internal shutdown, but risk in itself is but a prompt to examine an uncertain situation in new light.

Understanding uncertainty

Academics like Frances Milliken have identified that uncertainty consists of three different elements. Firstly, by its nature, you don't know what it is that is going to happen and when it is going to happen. I think it is often the 'when' that is more important. We do know that climate change is happening; we just don't know when it will become catastrophic. For years, the inevitability of a pandemic has been understood, but 'when' was, until 2019, a mystery.

Secondly, you don't know how that unexpected change is going to impact you. The uncertain question is: 'Will global warming impact me personally, and if so, how much? Will it be a mild irritation or life-threatening?'

As someone once said to me – a Brit:

> 'Global warming? Well, at least we might get some decent summers!'

And thirdly, you may be uncertain about how well you could *respond* to this unexpected change with unexpected impacts upon you! It is this response to uncertainty that shapes how we deal with an Impossible World.

Responding to uncertainty

It is worth thinking about how you respond to uncertainty. How do you face fear? Are you one of the following?

- **Risk Avoider** – Someone who withdraws from risk, hoping that someone else will bear the burden for them. They sidestep challenge and uncertainty at all costs, preferring a false sense of security over the discomfort of growth. But this reliance on external protection leaves them powerless when that protection is removed.

- **Risk Embracer** – A thrill-seeker, the cliff-jumper, the free-falling junkie of life. For them, risk is not just necessary; it is the reward itself. They chase the adrenaline high of pushing themselves to the edge and revel in the challenge of coping. Risk is their playground, not their prison.

- **Risk Taker** – The ones who engage with uncertainty not because they seek the thrill, but because avoiding it would mean denying who they are. They take risks because to do otherwise would stop them from being who they want to be and doing what they want to do. They accept risk as the price of admission for a life fully lived – the unavoidable terms of doing business with reality. You might also call them risk managers.

It may well be that in different situations you feel your relationship to uncertainty is different. In which case it can be interesting to ask yourself: what are the consequences, costs, and benefits of this?

Risk Avoidance

There are specific situations where what seems to be risk avoidance can be the most rational stance to take. I may have an allergic reaction to certain foods found in many restaurants in which case avoiding a meal out is a reasonable position to take. But there is also the possibility this is likely to be a risk-taking opportunity where I might identify 'safe places to eat' to gain the benefit of eating out with friends whilst minimising the threat.

However, one of the most troubling potential consequences of risk avoidance is when it not just curtails our freedom but places the responsibility for risk protection totally on others, creating a dangerous dependency. There are those who refuse to engage with uncertainty, expecting someone else to completely shield them from it, whether that is the government, corporations, or institutions. The unspoken assumption is that risk can be outsourced – someone, somewhere, must keep us safe. But what happens when that protective force is withdrawn?

Look at how President Trump abruptly abandoned Europe, withdrawing America's traditional protective stance. European nations that had long relied on US defence policy found themselves exposed, forced to grapple with the realisation that their safety had been dependent on an external force rather than their own resilience. This is the risk-avoider's dilemma: dependency creates weakness, and weakness invites danger.

None of this is to say that others don't have a duty of care towards people and to keep people from harm. But as an adult might we not expect that someone also is mindful of the risks they are taking and acts responsibly within that knowledge?

Risk avoidance is, at its core, a psychological mix of the child and the servant mindset. The child assumes that a responsible adult will always be there to take care of them. The servant assumes that someone else – some higher authority – knows best. Both perspectives are based on an unrealistic outsourcing of responsibility. But the truth remains: nobody can eliminate risk for you. It is an inescapable fact of existence, and the sooner we accept this, the more empowered we become.

Risk Embracers

Risk Embracers are individuals who see risk as an end in itself, a chance to test themselves against the uncertainty of great challenge. They chase the adrenaline high. Often, according to the psychologist Mihalyi Csikszentmihalyi, this pursuit often aims to produce an internal state of flow – a state of high positive arousal in which an individual feels right at the edge but not exceeding their sense of competence or control. The simple formula is: the greater the risk and the more I feel I can cope with it the better. Soldiers facing that most uncertain of situations, a battle, have often reported feel exhilaration, even joy, as they face death or serious wounding.

These moments in extreme sports, battle and similar situations are incredibly intense and short lived and don't exactly offer a model for how we might deal with the ongoing uncertainty that we face on a day-to-day basis.

Risk Taking

In an uncertain world risk taking becomes an essential life skill. It is the means by which you survive and thrive. In losing our ability to take risks we are culturally losing an important element of our mental health toolkit, the ability to flourish with fear and to manage it in the cause of doing something worthwhile.

The ability to cope with risk and uncertainty is like a muscle – one that atrophies through disuse. If we do not engage with the unknown, if we do not challenge ourselves, we lose the resilience required to navigate a world that, by its very nature, is unpredictable. And herein lies the paradox: by attempting to eliminate risk, we make ourselves more vulnerable to it. This has serious implications for mental wellbeing.

Risk takers walk the path with open eyes, knowing that uncertainty is not an obstacle but a condition of life itself.

Risk taking is about having a sense of agency in regarding the unknown and the unknowable. It is knowing you have the choice – not to eliminate the risk, nor to suffer it passively, but to choose how you engage with it. It is to see what you can control and what you cannot, taking the responsibility to define for yourself how you involve yourself. As you will see, this is about standing back from the fear and anxiety, tapping into your natural resilience, recognising the potential of your individual psychodiversity and rewilding yourself to discover resources you didn't know you had.

Perhaps the real question is not whether we have become afraid to be afraid, but whether we have the courage to reclaim our ability to engage with risk, to lean into uncertainty, and ultimately to live with it in an abundant and flourishing way. So, you might begin by asking how we might have lost this resilient ability to deal with uncertainty in the first place.

Chapter 3: How We Got Here

It was 1991, and I was working, at the time, at what was then called the British Institute of Management. We got involved in a project to provide leadership training for managers in East Germany, sponsored by the British Ambassador in Berlin. I guess the idea was as the inevitable crumbling of the communist era accelerated, building relationships with the people who would help to regenerate the then-broken economies was a wise political move.

The result was that about sixteen economists and engineering company managers from East Germany came over to spend some time in the UK. As a result, I found myself one night driving home with Franz, an engineer, to take him to the nearby JCB factory the following day.

It was a lovely evening, and the sun was going down. We chatted convivially in the car, but then he grew sad. I asked him, 'What's the matter, Franz?' And he replied, 'This is terrible, isn't it, this?' I said, 'What's terrible?' He replied, 'So many fences, fields with walls, so many gates. People can't go anywhere.'

Now, what I was looking at was the bucolic whimsical loveliness of England on a summer's night. What he was seeing was a vision of elitism and oppression. The thought stayed with me. What we see is what we expect to see. And I do admit there are times when I look at the enormous gates of the rich houses, and I think perhaps Franz has a point!

If we want to develop our ability to deal with uncertainty, lessen our sense of helplessness and use fear productively, it is really useful to understand how we have become who we are, and what will be our starting point: how evolution and upbringing shape our relationship with the world.

We are all programmed to see the world in a particular way. We are shaped to filter out much of the available data of our perception. Our evolution as a species and the family, community, and society into which we are born shapes our understanding of the world. Essentially the result is a tribal perspective of life. This filtering brings to the foreground things that matter to the tribe (like the fences and gates above) and sends to the background that which is deemed unimportant.

Who Are We? The Weight of Inheritance and Expectation

We like to think of ourselves as independent thinkers, charting our own course through life, making rational choices based on free will. But in reality, who we become is shaped by two powerful, often invisible forces: our evolutionary inheritance and the expectations that form through culture, social learning, and personal experience. We do not enter the world as blank slates, nor do we move through life with unbounded autonomy. Instead, we are the products of inherited instincts and deep-seated patterns of belief that shape how we think, behave, and react.

While these forces have historically ensured our survival, they also limit us. The same mechanisms that once helped us thrive in close-knit tribes now constrain our ability to adapt, change, and think independently. The way we are brought up can grind away at our possibility for change, our potential to flourish in uncertain times.

In many ways, we are less free – and less resilient – than we assume.

The Evolutionary Shaping of the Mind

I remember vividly my first visits to the Atlas Mountains, where I spent time among the Berber people. Life there is communal in a way that feels both ancient and enduring. Water is shared through a complex system of communal channels, with each farmer having access on different days of the week. The muleteers, essential for trade and transport in the rugged terrain, elect a captain who allocates work fairly among them. Even the local Kasbah, often mistaken by tourists as a fortress, is actually a shared storage space – a place of security, yes, but also a testament to collective resilience.

Their strength lies in collaboration, a deep-rooted expectation that everyone plays their part. Over centuries, despite attempts by Arab and French rulers to control them, the Berbers have maintained their way of life. This was not due to military might or economic power but because of the powerful cohesion that comes from shared beliefs and social expectations. Their world is structured by an understanding that life is not about individual success but about the survival of the group.

This kind of thinking – tribal thinking – has dominated the way humans see the world for most of our history. Evolutionary psychology suggests that our brains have been shaped not for objective reasoning but for survival within a community. What mattered most was not abstract truth but the ability to work together, to understand and predict the intentions of others, and to fit into the expectations that bound the group together.

For early humans, this was a brilliant system. It gave us cooperation, shared knowledge, and the ability to build cultures. But it also created a deep reliance on inherited expectations. We evolved not just to survive in the world but to survive in our tribes. This is still the case today – we seek belonging, we fear exclusion, and we absorb the beliefs of those around us, often without questioning them.

Likely later in human history, as the shift from hunter-gathering to farming accelerated and communities increased in size, then ideas of status and leadership would have evolved – ideas about who is in charge and who is responsible became woven into the social fabric of the tribe. We began to develop servant mindset.

A Servant Mindset

This shaping starts with our parents and then continues with our teachers and other educators. And finally, this becomes, in our teenage years, the peers, the friends, the friendship groups that we know, and with whom we identify. This is one of the most potent processes we ever experience in our lives. It helps us function in the complicated, complex worlds to which we are born, but it can also take us hostage, distorting our view of the world around us and ourselves. It creates a 'servant mindset', determining what we pay attention to, what we believe and how we behave.

You may be uncomfortable with this, but the chances are that at least in part, you have a servant mindset. A servant mindset shows itself when you feel obliged to meet the expectations of others whether you want to at that moment. And we do this because we have allowed or assumed that person has the power to punish us directly or emotionally. We don't tell our boss the truth because he might reprimand us; we tell our partners what they want to hear to avoid upset, even if this means us being untruthful or avoiding saying something important. As mentioned, the gaolers of guilt, regret, and fear keep us in our place.

It can be a fear of criticism or condemnation. For when we allow someone to judge us, we give that person power. A power that continues long after the judge has forgotten we even existed. This giving up of power is what we exchange for safety and protection; at its worst, it takes us hostage.

Too strong a term? Well, think about what hostage essentially means. When you are taken hostage by threat or restraint, you are not free to choose your course of action. Or more insidiously – what to believe. We may even come, as did those taken hostage in a bank raid in Stockholm in 1973, to love our captors.

The psychologist George Kohlrieser is also one of the world's leading hostage negotiators. For him, there are striking similarities between the predicaments many people find themselves in their everyday lives and the situation that a hostage finds themselves in when they have been captured: He suggests that one of the early and biggest impacts of being taken hostage is an overwhelming sense of powerlessness. And that we can feel powerless, not just through physical restraint, but also in difficult situations involving emotional conflict. Powerlessness is like a poison that produces a deep, ongoing, and negative perception of reality. (*Hostage at the Table*, 2006)

And when this happens, we have handed the power to decide what is happening to us to others. That, to me, is a killer point. Once we start to feel helpless, the unconscious primitive part of our brain kicks in, and we begin to see everything as a threat.

This is even more likely in these turbulent times when the background anxiety levels of the world make us feel unsafe and threatened. Our evolutionary psychology will push us towards the safety of the group and its beliefs and its world view. We look for leaders and others to protect us and surrender our autonomy in return.

The Prison of Expectation

If evolutionary inheritance provides the foundation, this expectation building carves the details of who we become. Our minds are shaped not just by what we experience but by what we come to believe will happen.

David Robson, in *The Expectation Effect* (2022), highlights how our brains actively construct reality based on what we anticipate. A simple example is the placebo effect – people given a sugar pill but told it is a powerful painkiller often experience real pain relief because their brains release actual endorphins (Benedetti et al., 2005). The same principle applies to learning, performance, and even health. If we are told we are not good at something, we tend to fulfil that prophecy. If we believe we will succeed, we increase our chances of doing so.

The Pygmalion Effect (Rosenthal & Jacobson, 1968) demonstrated that teachers who believed certain students were more capable – regardless of actual ability – subtly encouraged those students to perform better. Expectations, even when unconscious, shape outcomes.

But what happens when the expectations we inherit limit us rather than empower us? Much of what we believe about ourselves – our abilities, our potential, our worth – is formed long before we have the chance to question it. Social structures and cultural narratives reinforce these beliefs, making them feel natural and unquestionable.

Starting large: becoming smaller

And there is the paradox of education and culture in preparing us for the world: we can start large and end up small. We are born rich in possibility, yet we can be blind to our potential.

We often lose sight of that potential. Our wholeself is curtailed. We start large like a marble block or the trunk of a tree, almost infinite in our possibilities, and end up sculpted into something more refined but missing a lot of material. And the sculptor is, for many years, not ourselves, but others. For many of us, it remains so.

Shaping, the process of growing up and becoming an adult is a process of narrowing down who we believe we are. Our beliefs about ourselves and the world become more limited. Much of this is useful. A young child's mind has been described as 'imperial': everything centres around 'me' and is a servant to it. We learn through our interaction with others that 'others' have needs and rights, which should be respected. We learn we are not immortal; we learn we are fallible. However, how we learn that can be critical.

For example, newborns can make every possible noise that underpins every possible language on the planet. They are language universalists, able to learn any sound needed to communicate in any language. But language you grow up with causes you to lose this acuity. Most of these sounds will be edited out and become very, very difficult, if not impossible, later in life to reproduce. For example, Japanese babies can hear the difference between the English sounds 'la' and 'ra', something most Japanese adults would find impossible.

Young children believe strongly in their potential. If you ask a child whether they can draw, the majority will say yes, quite confidently. If you ask an adult, most will say, 'No, I can't.'

The Cost of Tribal Thinking in a Changing World

One of the greatest challenges we face today is that while the structures of tribal life have broken down, the instincts they created remain deeply embedded in us.

I've seen this firsthand in both traditional and modern settings. In the Atlas Mountains, the Berbers maintain an unshakable communal identity, one that has resisted external influence for centuries. In contrast, in modern Western societies, traditional communities have fragmented. People are more mobile, social ties are looser, and yet, we still crave the same sense of belonging. But instead of village elders or community rituals, we turn to digital tribes – social media, political factions, ideological groups – that reinforce our biases rather than challenge them.

Google and Facebook, with their algorithms designed to keep us engaged, ensure that we mostly encounter ideas that confirm our existing beliefs. We become trapped in echo chambers, convinced of our own rightness, increasingly resistant to change. Neuroscientific research (Kapper et al., 2020) shows that when we encounter information that aligns with our beliefs, our brains reward us by strengthening those neural pathways. When confronted with contradictory evidence, however, we often fail to process it at all.

As David Ropeik notes in *How Risky Is It Really?*, 'We are social animals, instinctively reliant on a tribe for safety and protection. Any disloyalty literally feels dangerous, like the tribe will kick you out.' This explains why ideological shifts – whether political, religious, or personal – can feel like existential crises. The need to belong often outweighs the need to be right.

I carry my evolutionary inheritance and that predisposes me to deal with the world in a particular way but of course each of us is much more than that. Our problem-solving comes with a pre-installed operating system, our evolutionary inheritance, but the software and apps which make us unique and shape the world are the stories and expectations.

If we are to move beyond the limitations of inherited and given beliefs, we must first recognise how deeply they shape us. We must become conscious of how expectation moulds experience, how belief constrains perception, and how tribal instincts govern our sense of belonging.

Breaking free does not mean rejecting everything we inherit – it means questioning it, testing it, and consciously deciding what we accept and what we discard. This requires natural resilience:

We are not blank slates, nor are we fully independent thinkers. We are the sum of evolutionary inheritance and expectation, shaped by the communities into which we are born, and the beliefs we unconsciously absorb. While these forces have provided order and cohesion, they have also made us less autonomous and less resilient in the face of change.

Understanding how we are shaped – how our brains filter reality, how expectations dictate experience, and how tribal instincts keep us tethered to inherited beliefs – is the first step toward reclaiming true agency. The next step is harder: actively choosing who we want to be.

For this, you need to start examining the *story you tell about yourself*.

Chapter 4: The Story So Far

I'm a soldier and a mystic,
A baker and a thief.
I could be a carpenter,
That is my belief.

Who is summoned when you ask yourself the question 'Who am I'? How do you know who you are? This might seem an odd question, but how you see yourself is surely a starting point for having a change in your relationship with yourself and the world.

Who is the 'me' that faces this Impossible World? The unique stick-like 'I' that emerges from the inheritance of evolution and the spider's web of significant moments and expectations that have become woven around you since you were born? The 'I' that must turn to face an Impossible World?

The 'I' is often told as a story. As a psychologist I have always paid close attention to the stories people tell about themselves. They often serve as explanations as to why a particular person feels something, always does something, why they believe what they believe. Listening, you can start to see a rich picture of how life is understood and enacted by that person often captured as a kind of meta-narrative, repeated and replayed in various forms as a deep explanation of how and why they 'are'. Reflecting on your own story, your unique evolutionary and shaping journey, understanding it, and recognising how it moulds your expectations and reactions is the first step to liberation.

Your story is drawn from many sources: at school gates, in the bars of pubs, in office canteens, classrooms and playgrounds, old infantry regiments, chapels, mosques and temples. The gossip grows and whole lives of individuals – once grey and roughly sketched – become drawn rich and round, grotesque and grandiose, deceitful, and divine. Misadventures found discarded in the waste bin of passing time – and belonging to someone else – are recovered and glued onto this portrait of a 'you'. You gather explanations and reasons like headscarves, jewellery, a hanging bag, a feather, and a broken heart. Some of these are added by other people, and others drop unnoticed into the dirt.

Some of the tales that illuminate the whole are true in a kind of arbitrary way and placed centre stage; and others, which might have been a better illustration, are lost or denied. And so, this someone becomes you dressed in suppositions, assumptions, judgements, rumours, cartoons, and calico. It becomes your 'identity'.

An interesting question arises: to what extent is your identity that which constitutes the unique phenomena which is 'I', a fixed point, and how much is a work in progress?

To explore this, we need to think about how we come to build this complex, multi-layered phenomenon which is summoned up when we asked the question 'who am I?'

In answering this we will often answer first with a collection of labels: tall, rich, anxious, vegetarian, overweight, deaf, divorced, creative, fuzzy, laid-back, doctor, musician, and so on. And then if we ask why or how we are like this we will provide a story, the primordial soup from which our identity by and large has emerged. I call these 'I am/because' stories.

- I am afraid of heights because I was stuck on a cliff as a child.

- I am a songwriter because my grandfather wrote funny monologues and played the harmonica in the clubs of northern England.

- I am unfit because I have a bad knee.

And then there are variations on this pattern:

- I didn't sing for years because I was told by my mum that I sang like my dad, whose relationship to the strictures of a well-tempered Bach was somewhat cavalier.

- I didn't get that job because I didn't go to Oxbridge.

- I am a believer in independent thinking because my father was a contrarian.

These are the stories I tell about myself. I guess that, most likely, there is some grain of truth in the historical event itself, but overall, the assumptions that are taken in that word 'because' may well be dubious.

One thing all stories do is draw a line of explanation through a chaotic cluster of events. Somehow out of the chaotic and almost infinite, we simplify our explanation of life to make it narratively efficient. 'Because' is a choice – and often a partial and arbitrary one; a selection that ignores or does not see other possibilities. Yet once chosen this 'because' explanation doesn't need repetition to become almost unbreakable. So often it just needs narrative plausibility.

It is like those Agatha Christie-type stories when the cast of characters gather in the library and the eccentric detective runs through a series of events that have happened to lead him or her to show that the dreadful murder was committed by the mousy solicitor in the bow tie and everyone in the room is instantly sold on this account. But I have sometimes wondered amongst the red-herrings, diversions, and false trails through which we have travelled whether someone else might just be the guilty party if we take away the omnipotent pen of the author!

Whatever their validity, these stories lie at the core of how we see ourselves. This is the incredible power of the stories we tell or are told and our ability to survive and thrive in an Impossible World is by and large determined by them.

And potential for self-destruction is also captured in them. For many people it is probably easier to give up on the truth than give up on the story. If we want to understand a world in which millions of people believe the that Bill Gates was injecting millions of people with microchips in COVID vaccinations, that self-evident lawbreaking did not occur on election day, that several of your neighbours believe they have been abducted by aliens, then we need to appreciate the power of the story that ensnares them.

And even more so for a few, the sense of identity created in the crucible of a story is worth more than life itself. Those who die as martyrs for a cause are carried along by the story, for to give up the story is harder than dying.

Such is the power of a story. This is not to say that it is a bad thing, but to remind ourselves that the 'I', which I so strongly believe in, is a story.

But as suggested above the stories are not those of ourselves alone; they are the stories we got told by others about who we are and about the world we live in. They are how the expectations we have of the world and ourselves are captured and sustained.

Stories act like software programming: they determine what we pay attention to, our emotional response to events, the decisions we make and the actions we take. Once established they are fundamental to our way of dealing with the world. They are incredibly difficult to undo and we can become trapped in them.

Many of today's therapeutic approaches focus on untangling the stories we tell of ourselves and the act of interpretation that underpins them. Narrative Therapy, Cognitive Behavioural Therapy (CBT) and Acceptance and Commitment Therapy (ACT) all use the idea of exploring the stories we tell as a basis for intervention.

Sometimes the story becomes 'unremembered', buried in our unconscious or overlaid with other stories. But it still remains active, often signified by the labels we use to describe identity and capable of triggering our emotions, perceptions and giving power to our beliefs.

This is not to say that our identity is not to a significant extent determined by our genetic inheritance and early learning and socialisation into a particular culture but that we have a chance and choice to make about how much and to what extent we can be the authors of our own story. An abundant life should be based on the idea of a possibility of both changing the story so far and shaping the story to come.

Do I believe I can change?

And therein lies another key question in dealing with an Impossible World: do I believe I can change myself? Do I believe I can write a different story about who I am, one that enables me to change the things I can change?

If you believe you can write your own story you become the next level of supercomputer – a self-programming one.

As I face an Impossible World do I think the story of who I am is fundamentally complete or is it a work in progress? Or in other words, do I believe my identity is fixed or something that is evolving?

People often believe their identity is a fixed, static essentially unchanging thing, defined by a different set of characteristics often seen as being determined by biology, genetics, culture or early childhood. Who I am is fundamentally ingrained and unchangeable.

People who see identity as something more fluid and dynamic recognise who they are as being something that is being constantly shaped and reshaped in the light of experience and personal agency – something that they can take decisions about. This idea that who we are is something under construction was given prominence by psychologists such as Eric Erickson in the 1960s, who undertook a series of longitudinal studies mapping out how identity developed over a lifespan.

More recently this distinction has been echoed in the work of Carol Dweck[2] who distinguished between a fixed and growth mindset. She suggests that people can either believe their abilities and intelligence are statically unchangeable or as malleable and capable of improvement through effort and learning. She emphasised the importance of adopting a growth mindset to foster resilience, learning and personal development, ultimately shaping one's identity in positive ways.

You might wonder why so many people are so invested in the idea of identity being a fixed point. Surely if we are struggling to cope with the Impossible World, and accept that our ability to control external factors is limited at best, then not to think we can change ourselves is surely a counsel of despair?

But this is to miss the power of the story. Perhaps even the most 'fixed identity believer' accepts that they can take

---

[2] *The Growth Mindset*, Carol Dweck, 2017

different actions and exhibit different behaviours. The trouble is these are surface changes and are difficult to stick with without changing the values, beliefs, assumptions we have of ourselves.

A belief in our fundamental unchangeability in a complex and often chaotic world is reassuring and simplifying, providing a sense of structure, stability, and certainty. We have a need for an ongoing sense of self. This is why those story-based labels mentioned earlier feel so close to who we are.

In some cases, they may be examples of 'identity fusion'. I once heard a radio discussion about cochlear implants and how they could enable people with long-term, moderate-to-severe deafness to hear sounds and understand speech. I was intrigued by the debate in which some deaf people had said they wouldn't have the procedure. Being deaf, some of them felt, was part of who they were. It bound them at a deep emotional level to a group (deaf people) to the extent that the boundaries between personal identity and group identity were blurred. Individuals felt a strong sense of oneness with the group and were rewarded by a deep sense of belonging which in turn ensured strong commitment, sacrifice, and loyalty. This fusion of personal and group identity can also be found with sports teams, political movements, religious groups, and social causes. It is as if we have seen a feature of our evolutionary psychology.

This resistance to the idea of the evolving self can also be shown in the reluctance some of us have to give up our phobias and fears. This paradoxical attachment to something that makes us uncomfortable or even feel threatened can arise because it is something we have become familiar with; it provides a constant sense of who we are in a time of high change. The phobia may be held as a coping mechanism to deal with underlying stress, trauma, or unresolved issues. Holding onto it may provide a sense of control or predictability in our lives. Lastly, it can be a way of ensuring attention and support and even connection with others who have similar experiences.

How do we loosen up a story?

Most of the stories you tell about yourself may be fine and workable, helping you relate to the world in productive and satisfying ways. They are the stories that make you helpless or anxious or limit your life in some way. They are the stories that you might want to loosen your grip on, in order that you might engage in a more abundant, full life.

The first step might be to create a list of what you think you like and what you don't like. And what you think you can do and what you think you can't do. Ask yourself 'what is the story behind that particular like/dislike or can do/can't do'. Ask yourself how that story came to be? Now ask yourself in what ways might that story be selective, incomplete, or even untrue.

Let in a bit of possibility for an alternative account, a new story.

The early 20th century psychologist Alfred Adler believed that individuals have the capacity to imagine themselves in alternative situations and act 'as if' those situations were real. By acting 'as if' you were the person you aspire to be, you can change your attitudes and behaviours, and ultimately your life. I always found this an incredibly proactive and positive stance. In taking control of your story and becoming captain of your ship, when you act 'as if' the narrative you write is one of change and potential.

And all this starts with an acceptance that we are more than where we've ended up. We have possibility. Our possible self is waiting to be uncovered.

Part Two:
Solid Ground

Chapter 5: Natural Resilience

Recognising the story so far, where do you go from here? How do you unlearn your helplessness, how do you begin to more independently author your own story? How do you liberate yourself in this Impossible World? The next four chapters look at the resources we all have to renew our relationship with the world: our natural resilience, our psychodiversity and our ability to stand above the stream of events that flow around us and wonder 'what the hell is going on' and ultimately rewild ourselves. In short, how can we lose a servant mindset and begin to flourish?

And the good news is despite all the best efforts of our lords, masters, CEOs, religious leaders, dictators, and presidents-for-life we are not so very good at being servants anyway. Despite their best efforts – low wages, surveillance, intolerable conditions, frequent beatings, incarceration, and occasional mutilation – we keep wanting to do things our way, be ourselves, have control of our lives. Sometimes dangerously so. Take Zhao Gao, a civil servant during the Qin dynasty in old China. Passing the civil service entrance exam in those days included voluntary castration so it was as a eunuch he rose through the ranks to become a very senior member of the emperor's staff. He had the ear and mind of the old Emperor Zhaodi and when he died initially manipulated Emperor Huhai, making him a puppet ruler as he sought to consolidate his own power by having most of the Emperor's family executed for various dubious reasons. However, as Emperor Huhai began to assert his authority and seek independence, Zhao Gao, the not-so-faithful servant, orchestrated Huhai's assassination, installed a figurehead on the throne, thus gaining control over the empire without direct opposition, effectively ruling as the *de facto* leader.

This might be an extreme case, but we simply aren't as biddable and shapeable as our masters would want us to be – something that terrifies them. Too much of an expectation that we should be dutiful and ignore our self-interest and we tend to be like those French workers of old who would throw their wooden clogs into this new-fangled machinery when they felt they were being exploited. The French word for a wooden shoe is *sabot*, from which is derived the word 'sabotage'.

The inclination to rebel we will return to, but for now it is useful to remember that our inner mischievousness is an important part of who we are and a not just an irritating quirk best ignored by sensible people. We are not so biddable that we can't redefine ourselves and the world around us.

We may have a drive to belong but we also have a drive to break free. And we may have to break free from the rather dubious 'safety' of the master/servant relationship to in-source our ability to survive and thrive in this Impossible World.

To do that we may need to reclaim something vital for the task.

Discovering our Natural Resilience

In the course of this book so far, implicitly and explicitly, there is the notion that, faced with an Impossible World, we have lost – or at least in many cases eroded – something that is essential for us to survive and thrive. That something is resilience: being able to move through the chaos and unpredictability of the world with balance, and a sense of lightness of being. We need to develop a resourcefulness that helps us bounce back from setbacks, deal with the unexpected, take risks, deal with disappointment.

When you look around at how the idea of resilience is often discussed it can sound like something learned in a sweaty gym. It's almost a competitive thing about being tough, mentally fit, lifting the psychological weights, the goal is to *cope* with something that is out to get you. Resilience is something we can learn and train for.

But what if resilience is not something we learn and gain but something we forget and lose? Natural resilience is an innate part of who we are. A baby is born into a world that they will find impossibly random and unpredictable in its nature and yet she learns to thrive within it. An old lecturer of mine, Dr Peter Stratton, taught me children always would endeavour to make the best of the situation they are in, finding best fit solutions to the problems they face. (It is only later that these learnings become problematical as new situations arise demanding an unlearning of what went before.) From our earliest moments, we possess incredible coping mechanisms. Even as babies and toddlers, we seem to be able to move from the negativity to positivity, from misery to joy, from disaster to relief in seconds.

There's a familiar scene many parents will recognise. A baby is in distress – crying hard, completely overwhelmed. Their whole body is involved in the emotion. Then, suddenly, the crying stops. Their attention shifts. They catch sight of something, hear a sound, or feel a familiar touch. In moments, they are calm again. They may even smile, coo, or start to play.

To an adult, it can seem confusing. How can someone go from deep distress to delight in just a few seconds?

What we're seeing in that moment isn't emotional instability. It's something much more fundamental. It's a powerful example of what you might call *Natural Resilience* – the built-in, instinctive ability to move through disappointment and emotional disruption and return to a state of balance and engagement.

This kind of resilience is not taught. It's not the result of strategy or maturity. It's something we're born with. And in early life, it's remarkably visible.

Babies don't suppress their feelings, and they *don't cling to them either*. They express what they feel – fully and freely. But just as quickly, they let the emotion pass when the need is met or something new captures their attention. This ability to feel deeply and then move on isn't learned behaviour; it's a natural pattern, and one that continues to operate in all of us, even when we forget how to access it.

In that small moment – the quick shift from distress to recovery – we see emotional autonomy in its most basic form. The baby expresses distress not to manipulate or dramatise, but because something in their environment isn't right. But when things settle, or something new emerges, they often move on without hesitation. They don't return to calm reluctantly – they actively reclaim it. This isn't emotional passivity. It's a kind of agency. They will push, turn away, resist, wriggle, and signal displeasure! The baby is seeking to recover their balance, to move back toward a state of comfort and positive engagement with the world. They are not just surviving the moment but moving through it. Overcoming adversity for a young child is not a return to a passive calm state, but feeling able, actively and completely, to involve themselves with the world.

That process, however, doesn't happen in isolation. The baby's system is supported by connection. A voice, a gentle touch, or simply the presence of a familiar caregiver helps regulate their nervous system. Babies don't just calm themselves by force of will – they calm *through connection*. What's more, they don't simply receive this comfort passively. They actively seek it. They turn their heads toward the sound, reach for the person, settle into the rhythm of breath and body. Their recovery is supported by someone else's presence, but they are also participating in that connection. It's a co-created moment of safety.

Then something beautiful happens. Once the distress fades, the baby looks outward again. Moving on, they explore. They reach for a toy, track a light, test their voice. Their curiosity reawakens. This isn't just distraction: it's a return to the world. They are reasserting interest, rebuilding engagement. Resilience doesn't just mean ending distress. It means resuming exploration and reclaiming the world with a sense of openness.

And as they re-engage, the baby begins to experiment. They make sounds, reach and grasp, react to faces. These small acts of trial and error are not random. They are part of a natural process of emotional and cognitive rebuilding. Through movement and sound, the baby is regaining a sense of control, learning how their actions affect the world, and tuning themselves to their environment. This is how recovery deepens, not just through calm, but through action. They reassert their wellbeing. They are 'wholehearted'.

Even in the youngest infants, we can also see the first signs of imaginative reframing. A baby who moments ago was distressed may become entirely absorbed in a flickering shadow, a sound, a shifting pattern of light. They don't need words to reframe the moment. They do it through attention, sensation, and fascination. They are no longer just *not upset;* they are discovering something new; they are learning to see a situation in new ways. The feeling changes, and so does the meaning of the moment. It is this arc of recovery to renewal that to me captures what it is to be naturally resilient.

Taken together, these observations tell us something simple but profound: resilience doesn't arrive later in life as a skill we have to acquire. It begins here. In movement, in connection, in attention, in exploration. We are born with the capacity to recover, reconnect, and reengage.

Of course, life becomes more complex and we experience disappointment, shame, and the long drag of memory. As we age, we learn to filter our emotions, to hide them or hang onto them but never let them go. Whereas a baby seems in most circumstances seems to be able to fully experience an emotion and let it go and move on, we bottle up the tendency to hang on and even nurture it. What we see in a baby's quick recovery is not a trick of development or a sign of emotional immaturity.

It's a demonstration of something deeply adaptive in the human system – a built-in capacity to begin again, again and again. And as adults, we don't need to build it from scratch. We need to *recover* it and find our way back to the rhythm we once knew so well.

The ability to move through emotional disruption, restore balance, and re-engage positively with the world is already within you. It was always there. These buildings blocks of resilience – autonomy, connection, exploration, experimentation, and imagination – are at the core of how you can survive and thrive in an Impossible World. We will return to them in Part Three as we explore five practices or 'rules of the road' for a more liberated life.

In recent years, the idea of resilience has become central in psychology, education, health, and leadership. Most commonly, it's described as the capacity to adapt, recover, and keep going in the face of adversity and challenge. The focus is often on traits like grit, perseverance, cognitive flexibility, and emotional regulation.

This understanding of resilience can be useful. It offers practical tools for navigating difficulty and recognises that our responses to stress can be shaped and strengthened over time. But the danger, if it is too simplistically adopted, is that resilience becomes seen as a pugilistic approach captured in the language of the gym or the sports arena. The idea of innate natural resilience is more akin to that of an improvisational dancer moving through challenge and adversity in a creative and exploratory way.

Where the 'learned' model tends to focus on *techniques we can use to recover*, natural resilience starts with *what we are naturally equipped to do*, before any instruction or strategy is introduced.

It would be easy to set these two approaches against each other – as if we had to choose between them. But they are not in opposition. They are, in fact, *different parts of the same story*.

Natural resilience provides the foundation. It shows us that resilience is not something we need to learn, but something we can return to. It is a reminder that recovery and adaptation are part of our biological and relational wiring – not external achievements, but internal capacities that emerge naturally.

In this way, we can begin to see resilience not as either innate *or* learned, but as *both innate and learnable*. We start with the embodied, relational capacity for recovery, and over time, we build on it. We shouldn't lose sight of our natural resilience as we grow.

Recognising both parts of this picture helps us respond more compassionately, both to ourselves and others. It means we avoid treating resilience as a performance or an achievement or something that can be outsourced to others and begin to understand it as a layered capacity: something that begins in the body, is shaped by experience, and can be supported by both connection and conscious practice.

In one way you might see what follows as ways of reawakening the natural rhythms of recovery and discovery we knew instinctively in early life. Natural resilience is enabled by embracing your psychodiversity: the whole, complex system that is 'you' (Chapter 6); developing the mindset that focuses on what you can do rather than what you can't (Chapter 7); and then learning the profound lessons of the way nature itself restores its ability to regenerate and renew (Chapter 8).

Servant no more.

Chapter 6: The Possibility of You

On the face of it, my father was a pillar of the local community. He was a surveyor with his own practice, with a reputation for honesty, straightforwardness, and intelligence. Scotland Yard used him as an expert witness in fraud cases. He was a president of the local Rotary; he sat on the board of the local Regional Health Authority; he was commodore of the yacht club. His actions often seemed to be motivated by a deep sense of civic duty. In a crisis, he stepped up.

People said of him that he was a good man. He was serious and thoughtful and extremely hard working. Perhaps he had a reputation for being too serious, and maybe a little dry.

In a book about the housing association which he helped found, the author notes that many colleagues were surprised and delighted when he revealed a hitherto hidden streak of fun at his leaving party. They should have known him better.

For the record, Dad was enigmatic, contradictory, mischievous, irritable, kind, frustrating, brave, awkward. And that was on a good day. A wholly unnecessary and private strain of rebelliousness ran like a constant thread throughout his life. It started early, as a three-year-old when he disappeared from the house and was missing for several hours. The police eventually found him returned to his panic-stricken parents having ridden his tricycle on his own over three miles along methodically remembered bus routes to the seaside because he wanted to go for a paddle.

At 11 years old, he had the second-highest marks in the county in his exams and a place at the prestigious Portsmouth Grammar school, which he turned down to go to the local school with his brother. Gaining very high marks in his School Certificate at 16, he was told by everyone he was going to follow in the footsteps of his eminent uncle Benjamin Carter, a brilliant research engineer and the real inventor of the jet engine! So, he elected to take arts subjects at Higher Certificate, which manifestly were not his forte. (His French accent was described later in life as belonging to an inarticulate peasant!)

He was a competitive yachtsman, winning many races, principally in the Irish Sea. Again, with a certain maverick tendency shining through. He used his superb knowledge of the weather to outthink his competitors tactically. My brother, being his loyal crew for many fierce races, recalls feeling disconcerted and embarrassed when on the sound of the starting gun, 25 yachts sailed off in one direction and one, the one he was on, sailed in precisely the opposite. He began to suspect that Dad did this, not just because of his better knowledge of the weather, but he knew it ruffled the competition.

He was a hard man to know, even for his son. He never spoke much about his life. Conversations for him were principally about debating issues to do with politics, ideas, history, science, and moral duty, not reflecting on the past. And that which I did know of him came mostly from my mother, who was often an unreliable witness. I do know that his mother had died when he was 14 and that he was evacuated during the war to avoid the massive bombing in Portsmouth. Of course, he refused to stay away and came back. He was left with his brother in the care of two elderly aunts, his father running a shop during the day, and doing war service at the waterworks during the night.

They were poor. My grandfather was not a successful businessman, and Dad, abandoning his studies, left home at 16 to live in London to train as a surveyor. Perhaps it was this that made him so firmly his own man. He was successful in business by working fanatically hard. On the face of it, he appeared solidly a member of the middle class, living in a middle-class house with a middle-class car, taking middle-class holidays. He himself brooked no desire to join this particular club. 'I am a member of the meritocracy,' he used to say, 'And so should you be.' His regard or disregard for people was independent of status, wealth or education and meant he never really fitted into any social group, despite his memberships.

Being his son was not easy. If he had ever been given a *How to Bring Up Your Son* handbook, he clearly lost it very soon in the early days. When I was eighteen months old and following the birth of my brother, Dad found himself in the terrifying position of looking after a very young boy. Now the kitchen was a foreign land to him, so after a few experiments around what this strange thing called his son might eat, he settled on pineapple jam, which he fed to me three times a day until my mother returned from the hospital.

He was unreliable, to say the least, in terms of attention and thought. Urged by my mother to spend more time with his sons, he took my brother and me down to London, where, at seven and nine years old, we spent a bewildering afternoon walking around the London Design Centre. This was a place he loved. In those days, it was full of spindly furniture of tubular steel, and pine, fabrics which brutally rejected the cottage-quaint of yore, unpatterned crockery, and mysterious chrome gadgets. Not a dinosaur or suit of armour was in sight.

Looking up some old photographs of the Design Centre, the title on one of them sums everything up:

> *A visitor to the Design Centre, consulting files on refrigerators, 1967.*

Forced upon return by my mother to discuss the itinerary of the day we had just experienced, a somewhat crestfallen father found himself taking us back down to London the following weekend for a more typical visit to the London Planetarium and the waxworks of Madame Tussauds.

Meals for him were to be a blend of my mother's excellent cooking and debate. He would take issue with almost any view expressed whether or not these contradicted previous statements of his own. He loved to argue, and that was that. I remember well one lunchtime. He always enjoyed listening to lunchtime news. A news item had focused upon the very left-wing Labour politician Tony Benn. As it finished, I saw him looking at me carefully. I decided a low-key swift lunch was what I needed, not an hour plus of political debate, so I said something vaguely disparaging about Benn. Dad had become quite right-wing with the years and had only the previous day been grumbling about the Labour party. Reasonably I thought this would let me continue undisturbed, eating my Mum's great roast potatoes. I was wrong.

> 'The trouble with you, Stephen,' he didn't hang around, making it personal, 'is that you can't distinguish

between the worth of a man and the worth of his particular arguments.'

'Dad!' I protested, 'You spent one and half hours arguing yesterday how the Labour party was insane!'

'And that they are,' he replied. 'But Mr Benn speaks his truth and says what he believes, and there are too few politicians on either side who do that! He may be quite mad, but he is also honourable and principled.'

I never knew in arguments like these whether he actually thought that, or it was just a point of discussion However, I have kept the lesson with me all my life since.

His complexity never dimmed. A man of firmly held values, he could be surprisingly liberal, something I did not appreciate at the time. On the news that his son was going to go to university to read philosophy and psychology, two subjects which, in those days, were guaranteed to lead to reasonably immediate unemployment, he did not say a word to convince me otherwise. A respect that every other person on my course had been denied. He very rarely told me what to do concerning issues, major and minor.

Towards the end of his life, you would find him complaining to the Cats Protection League that cats were bothering his garden and the birds therein. Or deliberately misunderstanding cold-calling insurance salespeople pretending he could not hear properly and demanding they stop trying to offer him a goat.

Two weeks before he died, he was on the church roof surveying the state of the building, to help organise its restoration.

Dad was never one thing *or* another – he was one thing *and* another. Walt Whitman once said, 'Do I contradict myself? Very well, then, I contradict myself. I am large. I contain multitudes.'

Dad also.

Containing Multitudes

I wrote more about my father then I anticipated. The more I remembered this 'serious' man, the more odd and contradictory he seemed. And I have a suspicion that if you reflect upon an important 'other' a similar contradictory picture will emerge. It seems certain that we are not all one thing *or* another, but rather one thing *and* another. The story we tell ourselves is one of a myriad possible selves.

Psychologically it is the world of possibility that lies within us all; it is a call towards who we could be, another life, another world. It is the magic 'quirk' of our evolutionary nature, scaring us and exciting us at the same time. However much we feel safe and secure, we cannot but look towards this other, weird world and wonder. This quirk is our contrariness – the mutation of all mutations – the God particle, perhaps. We cannot help ourselves; the rebel and revolutionary lies within us all, howsoever hidden and ignored. I have always found this a beautiful idea. Evolution has provided us with the tool for its undoing. We change our thinking; we change our feeling; we change our minds! Sometimes this is contingent on things that happen outside of ourselves: we learn something, and it changes our perceptions. But only an unobservant fool would pretend that it doesn't happen the other way around: we change our minds and then learn something to support this new way of thinking or feeling.

In Praise of Inconsistency

In the late 1990s, I met a remarkable man, Dr Michael J Apter. He is a collector of antique Americana, wrote the early definitive text on cybernetics, is a lover of jazz, and is fluent in French. He got married to his first wife in Versailles Palace. With his second, he ran a bar in Spain, and with the wonderful Mitzi, his third wife, he splits his time between Baton Rouge and New Orleans. His schoolboy friends include John Cleese. He is useless at golf. He is also possibly the most remarkable psychologist of his generation and has been visiting Professor at the Universities of Purdue, Chicago, Northwestern, and Georgetown.

Unlike virtually every other thinker at the time, he did not see people as defined as types or measured by traits. He recognised that people were fundamentally and individually *psychodiverse* and thus *inconsistent,* and *changeable*, and capable of every emotion, and every motivation. We differ, according to Mike, in the amount of time we spent in different motivational states, but we all experience all eight of them. So, we are motivated to achieve things and to enjoy something for just what it is, enjoy the moment if you like. We are motivated to fit in and do what is expected of ourselves, but we are also, on other occasions, mischievous, rebellious, cantankerous, and reluctant to follow the line. We want to be in control and feel competent, but we also are happy sometimes to enable others to be in control and to be competent. And lastly, we want to be cared for and liked, but we also really, really want to care for and like others. These, he calls different 'motivational states,' and they are summarized below.[3]

---

[3] In different discussions about Reversal Theory the names of the motivational states might be labelled differently and set out in a slightly different way. For ease of explanation, I have used this framework.

We are motivated to:

- Achieve things, from the simply practical to the awesome

- Belong and fit in, feel part of the team or community

- Control, feel competent and skilful, to master

- Be compassionate, show people our friendship, love and concern

- Enjoy ourselves, do things for the sheer pleasure of doing them, for their own sake

- Break free, do our own thing, not follow the herd

- Enable others to gain skills, learning, understanding

- Seek affection, feeling liked, loved and looked after

The story of our lives is captured in both how much time we spend in each of these states and how successful we are at being in them. For instance, my need to achieve may become a constant source of anxiety, or playfulness something we feel awkward about and deny ourselves. We may lose the confidence to belong or lack the courage to break free. We may feel we are not good anything or embarrassed about helping others. We may feel lonely or unlikable or unloved even or be too shy to express our care and feelings for others.

But to develop the skills and understanding and behaviours that enable us to gain satisfaction in these states opens up an almost limitless world of possibility for us. And not only because, when an opportunity arises, we have the means to respond well to that opportunity, whether it is to achieve something or enjoy ourselves, but also because we can choose how to engage with a particular situation in different ways. You might feel that particular moment does not afford much opportunity for playful enjoyment but you could reframe it as an opportunity to help others (enable) or to show solidarity with those involved (belonging).

What's on offer here is a dynamic existence – life is a game for dancers not statues.

And Mike's genius was to see that these motivational states are opposites and that we switch between them, what he calls a 'reversal.' This happens often unconsciously and without deliberation. One example would be when we are focused on getting something finished, looking for a sense of achievement but get bored and start looking at Facebook or make ourselves a drink, seeking enjoyment. Another would be after a day of caring for our children (caring for others), we sink into a chair and pour ourselves a drink (caring for self). Now what is interesting is that Mike Apter's research shows that any particular motivational state is not wholly dependent upon the situation you are in, which is why in a 'serious' meeting at work you might find yourself feeling any of those other states.

You might become mischievously bored wanting to feel free and enjoy yourself. You might feel sorry for someone else who is being humiliated by the boss, wanting to care for them.

Our experience of life at any moment will be made up of a mix of these motivations with one or two being more vital at any one time. All of us are inconsistent: the hardened warrior hides behind the vulnerable little boy within (to master *vs* to be cared for); the manipulative coach hides their self-centredness (to enable *vs* to master); the prim Sandy in the film *Grease* suddenly appears as a liberated and confident woman (to belong *vs* to be free and rebellious).

What is remarkable about this is that he captures the whole of what it is to be a human and insists that all these elements make up our lives. This blew my mind. It still does. It is so apparent and so ignored at the same time. The purpose of our lives is not just to achieve things in the narrow sense of work and acclaim. This made visible is our 'wholeself', our blueprint for a wholehearted life. These motivational states underpin what we pay attention to in the world. Our experience of them shapes our emotions. Together they create purpose and passion.

Inhabiting our lives

The purpose of our lives is to inhabit well all these states. This is a richness of the subtle and beautiful kind. It suggests to me the idea of the 'wholeself' that recaptures and enriches the natural resilience we are born with and gives us the means to survive and thrive in an Impossible World as we develop the life skills and behaviours that arise from them. The psychodiverse 'wholeself' is an *abundant* one, and the means by which we can renew our relationship with the world and engage it with its tempestuous uncertainty.

What has been fascinating for me over the years is to watch how advances in our understanding of neuropsychology and evolution have increasingly confirmed the validity and utility of this. The conception of humans as being nothing but self-interested manipulators of their environment and others for selfish gain, often known by economists as 'economic man', has collapsed and been shown time and again to be neither right nor useful. Increasing research shows that the evolution of our brains predisposes us to be collaborative, playful, and empathetic and that an inclination towards being friendly and kind is the basis of our intelligence.

Consider this: there are two tribes in a landscape in which animals need to be hunted, dwellings built, crops grown, children looked after, accidents and catastrophes managed. One tribe is entirely constituted of self-interested individuals trading any contribution they make to the whole purely based on a reward to themselves. They would not be prepared to make one iota of input for which they do not believe they will be adequately rewarded. The other tribe is characterised by members who are ready to care for others as well as themselves, to teach others the things they have learned.

Members who can take responsibility for themselves are able to enjoy themselves and now and then break the rules if they see or think of a better way. It would be hard to argue that this tribe would not flourish and cope better than the one constituted of 'economic' men and women.

Similarly, a workplace, or a project, or a community constituted of members who felt able to contribute their 'wholeself' would be amazingly healthy, for each of these motivational states feeds the others. Caring for others builds trust and insight as well as reciprocity. Being free provokes challenge and questioning and innovation. Enjoyment creates energy and exploration; mastery endows a group with competence and control.

Yet the narrow-cold view of human behaviour as self-interested is still the dominant frame of reference, and it is tough to undo, especially in the context of work. The challenge for us is to let go of this view of ourselves. It is insidiously internalised.

The desperate and blind pursuit of achievement in an uncertain world is unlikely to help save you.

Goals and plans have a role to play, but not a pre-eminent one. You will have the best chance of being a resourceful human being by engaging your 'wholeself' in all that you do.

I am not suggesting here that you become unambitious. To strive to achieve great things is a noble human activity. *But* see it for what it is and make it meaningful and worthwhile. Do not fall into the self-deluded trap of thinking that you are pursuing this dream *in order to*, for example, care for others or enjoy yourself. The truth is that narrow ambition rarely delivers these things. As one senior leader told me, trapped in a contract that was running on for ever with the promise of a huge pay-out when it was completed:

> 'You know, the problem with money is that it costs too much!'

Many years ago, I ran a seminar for CEOs in businesses. There were some guest speakers. One came in his chauffeur-driven Jaguar from a very well-known global company. He was that morning's speaker. He addressed the group. 'Let's start by saying if you want to be successful, if you want to make a difference, you should know I'm estranged from my fourth wife, my daughter doesn't speak to me, I've had two heart attacks and had to spend Christmas day working with my boss.' I remember looking at him, thinking, 'You're the poorest man I've ever seen.'

Single-minded pursuit of achievement can be an addiction, in which you attain a brittle moment of triumph, pause oh-so-briefly, and set off again. In the meantime, all the other aspects of our 'wholeself' receive no attention and degrade. In the end, in the cruellest of ironies, we become less and less effective, because it is the abundant wholeself we need to flourish and succeed.

There will be short periods in your life when you might need to be single-minded, but treat this as a temporary strategy, and not as a lifestyle choice. Resourcefulness and resilience lie in embracing the paradox of who we are. The story you tell of yourself must be: 'I am many things, I am psychodiverse, I am changeable.'

Ralph Waldo Emerson once said:

> 'A foolish consistency is the hobgoblin of little minds, adored by little statesmen and philosophers and divines.'

The pressure to be consistent is powerful. Our friends tease us for our inconsistency, the press dig through the trash to prove our politicians do the opposite of what they say. Sometimes it can feel like the world enjoys nothing more than a game of 'Gotcha!'. We have a social horror of hypocrisy. We create rules for ourselves. Rules about what we like, what we eat, what we are good at, what we believe. And we feel we must stick to them.

But you need to demand the space to be inconsistent as a human right. Without that right, how can you change? Being inconsistent allows you to explore options about what to think, what to do, how to be. The simple truth is that what got you where you are today may not be the thing you need for the future.

Then there is the concept in cybernetic theory of 'requisite variety'. In it, the repertoire of behaviours and attitudes you have at your disposal must equal or exceed the often-conflicting demands of the environment you are in. Then you will thrive. Given that the current situation seems to have more than enough variety in it for most of us, then not restricting your options by a false need for consistency may be a wise move.

At the start of this book, I highlighted the idea that from Rutger Bregman about 'moral ambition'. We can now see the power of this as we find it in it the potential to meet the motivational needs for achievement, care for others, enablement, and possibly breaking free (in so much as it would challenge the social expectations often in play). This a noble and important call for action, but it does not necessarily address the need to playfully do things for their own sake, to be taken care of, or to belong. And yet these are the very things that would give us the strength to maintain our moral ambition and, indeed, to foster the skills that would help it succeed.

Living a motivationally rich life – a fulfilling life – is, I believe, our ultimate purpose. At its best, it lets true spirituality in. Living a life where we are aware of the paradox implicit within it; developing a holistic engagement with the world that integrates personal growth, empathy, creativity – and sees the interconnectedness of things – is a road to spiritual transcendence.

But to get there is no simple step between the narrow, servant-based life living in a whirlpool of social media, and constantly juggling expectations and the idea of living as your wholeself.

You need to lift your attention out of the noise, clutter and turbulence of everyday life and see the 'you' – the abundant self – that is waiting to be reclaimed. What stories could we then tell about ourselves?

Chapter 7: The Captain of Your Ship

I have always been a bit of an admirer of the ancient Greeks – apart from (of course) the slavery, misogyny, xenophobia, rigid class structures and the belief that farting was an expression of intellectual freedom.

At the core of a lot of their philosophy is often the question: how do I build a relationship with the world in which I am useful, moral, and reasonable? What is it to be fulfilled?

'The unexamined life is not worth living,' said Socrates a while ago. Not to question your beliefs about yourself and the world you live in, not to understand how you have been shaped and are being shaped still, but to expect to fit into the emerging Impossible World can be complacent, can it not?

Such thinking in Greek times wasn't something to be carried out in the gentle susurrus of some remote retreat or in a cave up in the mountains, but in the whirl and clamour of the marketplace – a place where, both metaphorically and practically, most of us live. The Greeks did practical philosophy you could *use*.

Picture this. It's 301BCE. Another sunstruck day in Athens, and the city square, the agora is alive with activity. The air is rich with the scent of olive oil, ripe figs, and the faint tang of the nearby sea, mingling with the warm earthiness of baked clay from pottery stalls. Overhead, swallows dart through colonnades, weaving in graceful airy pirouettes, while sparrows settle on the edge of the roof, pecking at stray crumbs and commenting on the scene The agora is surrounded by buildings, temples, and colonnades like the Stoa Poikile. People gather to shop at market stalls, listen to philosophers, and participate in civic life. Merchants have set up stalls to sell goods, artists and craftsmen display their wares, and citizens gossip, discuss the political headlines, plot and make decisions on important matters.

The Stoa Poikile itself, a long, shaded colonnade with one side open to the agora, provides cool respite from the harsh Mediterranean sun. Designed as a gathering place, it has rows of Doric and Ionic columns supporting a roof that shelters citizens from the midday heat. This colonnade is more than just a shaded walkway – it is a public 'room' where Athenians can stroll, talk, and engage in the city's social and intellectual life. Its name, 'Painted Porch,' comes from the murals along its interior walls, painted by renowned artists like Polygnotus. These vivid depictions of battles like the Battle of Marathon are reminders of Athens' glory and inspire a sense of civic pride, casting the space with both historical weight and beauty.

In this swirl of life stands the tall, gaunt figure Zeno of Citium, calm and steady amid the shifting sounds and scents of the city. Dressed simply, Zeno's lean frame blends into the crowd, yet his quiet authority draws people closer. He speaks plainly, talking about courage, patience, and learning to accept life's inevitable hardships. His listeners nod along, some leaning against the cool marble columns, others seated on the dusty steps. They're captivated – not by a grand performance, but by the way his words echo the simplicity of the natural world around them. Here, in the shade of the Stoa, in the busy business of the day, Zeno's teachings create a sanctuary of reason, a calm oasis where people can reflect on the art of living.

Zeno himself has had quite a life. He was born around 334BCE in Citium, a bustling port in Cyprus, where Greek and Phoenician influences met. Raised by a merchant father who encouraged his curiosity, Zeno grew up surrounded by diverse ideas. In his twenties, he made his way to Athens, where, legend says, he was shipwrecked and left with little but his determination. There, a chance purchase of Xenophon's *Memorabilia* ignited his passion for philosophy. He studied with Crates of Thebes, learning simplicity and self-sufficiency, and later with other teachers, blending ideas from various schools.

Gradually, Zeno developed his own philosophy. Establishing his school in Athens' Stoa Poikile (hence his followers are known as the Stoics) he has drawn people from all walks of life, teaching them to live virtuously, accept what they couldn't control, and find inner peace. His journey – from merchant's son to philosopher – shaped Stoicism, a philosophy that values resilience, wisdom, and ethical living.

They are an interesting bunch, the Stoic philosophers – they include an ex-slave (Epictetus), a Roman emperor (Marcus Aurelius) and a former advisor to Emperor Nero (Seneca). They all address a common challenge absolutely relevant to us today.

In the midst of a world that seems increasingly chaotic and unpredictable, how do you remain captain of your ship?

Or to put it another way, how do you create the mental space to embrace your wholeself and engage with the world in a new, more resilient, more fulfilling way?

At the heart of Stoicism is the idea that while you cannot control external events or the actions of others, you do have the power to control your responses and attitudes towards them. Ancient Stoic philosophers such as Epictetus and Marcus Aurelius taught that human beings are not disturbed by events themselves but by their interpretations of them. We may not control the storm, but we control how we steer the ship that is our own response and reaction. And the way we steer that ship is with wisdom, courage, justice, and temperance: the *wisdom* to know what you can control and what you cannot; the *courage* to hang onto what you stand for rather than surrendering to helplessness; the sense of *justice* asks us to treat others and the world ethically with fairness and respect, recognising the interconnectedness of everything; and finally the *temperance* to be moderate and thoughtful rather than being driven by extreme emotional reactions or desires.

What Zeno and his followers were proposing was what we would call cognitive reappraisal, dealing with unfolding reality in such a way that you create the space for your natural resilience to kick in and the inherent potential in your response to be engaged.

We don't always get to choose what happens to us. A meeting goes badly. A relationship frays. A plan unravels. Life, in all its unpredictability, throws us curveballs. But what if we could choose how we react? What if, instead of being at the mercy of events, we could stand at the helm, steering our own emotional ship?

Cognitive reappraisal – the skill of reshaping how we interpret and respond to life's challenges – isn't about denial or toxic positivity. It's about perspective. And it's something we can practise, just like a musician rehearses scales or an athlete refines technique.

This idea has deep historical roots in Stoic thought. This principle was echoed centuries later in modern psychology, particularly in cognitive behavioural therapy (CBT), pioneered by Aaron Beck and Albert Ellis. CBT introduced the idea that our thoughts shape our emotional world, and by changing our thoughts, we can change our experience of reality. Lately, scientists studying how emotions work – especially James Gross from Stanford – have found that how we think about a situation can really change how we feel about it. Gross, who leads the Stanford Psychophysiology Lab, has been a key figure in this research. He developed a model that explains when different strategies kick in to manage our emotions. Some strategies happen early on, like choosing to avoid a stressful situation or changing how you think about it (this is called cognitive reappraisal). Others happen later, like trying to hide how you're feeling (known as expressive suppression). Gross's work, especially in the *Handbook of Emotion Regulation*, shows that changing how you think about something *before* your emotions fully kick in usually works much better than just trying to bottle up your feelings. This aligns with Stoic principles, emphasising that our interpretation of events determines our emotional experience, rather than the events themselves.

The richness of psychodiversity suggested by Michael Apter's Reversal Theory builds on this in that we can reframe our experiences through the lenses of different motivational states. Thus, you might treat failing to get what you need (achievement) as a joke (playful). We might view the frustration you feel as your child refuses to do as they are told (mastery) as an expression of their fear or uncertainty (care for others). Or decide when group or a team doesn't welcome you as a member (belonging) as something you didn't want to join anyway (to be free of the obligations that would entail).

But this to do this requires a disengagement from our absorption with the unfolding noise and chaos of life. The ability to calm that noise and see beyond our assumptions to what is really going on and to the possibility within and without.

Stuck behind the wheel

I love sailing, particularly in the benign ancient waters of the Mediterranean. Being on a boat heeled over a stiff breeze, the sunlight sending diamonds and other jewels dancing behind in the wake, where grey islands like stone whales fall into azure waters feels like as good as life can get. A favourite place is sitting on the cabin roof watching: the shape of the sails; the horizon taking mental transit points to gauge our progress; the person behind the wheel checking they are happy and confident; keeping an eye on the changing courses of other vessels. Being mindful of the weather. It is in these moments that I feel genuinely the captain of my ship.

It is not behind the wheel, although I will do that for getting in and out of the harbour. Behind the wheel, you are stuck in one place; you cannot see the whole; you cannot communicate easily with other people; you cannot check the charts below. Don't get me wrong: I love taking the wheel and seeing how well I can get the boat to sail, but I have learned then I am not captaining the boat as well as I might be.

As a Captain you must have the awareness to craft the way the vessel sails, a hands-on feel for the wind, waters and the waves; you must be authentic, sure of yourself and comfortable in your skin and you need to be inspired – you must love the sea and accept its capricious and dangerous unpredictability. You must be able to stand back from the noise and immediacy of life's moment and gain distance and perspective. I would call this full attention.

And this is no less true if you want to captain yourself.

To be able to evaluate yourself objectively in a compassionate and non-judgemental way, you need to let go of the wheel now and again and watch how the ship of your life is sailing. And one thing is clear: no matter who has their hands on the wheel, only you can be responsible for the wellbeing of that ship and the course that it is on.

Finding Reflection

And this ability to look at yourself objectively is not immediately open to us all. What it requires is a level of maturity. It used to be thought that somewhere in your early 20s, everything stopped. Physical growth, personality, abilities, cognitive strengths, emotional intelligence, all kind of solidified. The brain itself was something about to experience a long and hopefully slow decline in which dying brain cells could no longer be replaced by new ones. Over the last few years, neurological, psychological, and behavioural research has shown that this is not true. The process of growing up is a lifetime's work; without effort, we might not complete it.

A psychologist called Robert Kegan focused on one aspect of this adult maturation, in this case, our relationship with our self.

When we are adolescents, we have what is called an *imperial* mindset. In this who we are is defined totally by our needs, our interests, and desires. A relationship with the rest of the world is purely transactional. For example, we do things or not because we perceive they will incur some reward or punishment rather than because they hold value for us.

Fortunately, most of us grow out of this stage and develop what he calls the socialised mind. In this, we define ourselves in terms of the relationships around us, in particular the shared ideas, norms, and beliefs in which we live. This is the process of shaping we have looked at already. Through it, we begin to take a view of ourselves based on how we feel others might see us. We can internalise this. If others see me as bad, then I must be. If others think I am a fool, then a fool I am. This shaped socialised mind needs the validation of others to feel whole. There is a constant seeking of affirmation: am I doing this right? Is this what you expect of me? What do you want from me? We seek to fit in. We want to belong. We do not question the things that we grew up with. We feel self-conscious; we feel guilty. Embarrassment keeps us in check. The people we cluster with are like us and need to be.

The next level in the evolution of self is what he calls the self-authoring mind. The self-authoring mind sees who 'I' am as a work in progress, something you can create, rather than something you are given by the tribe into which you are born. I am separate from my environment and the relationships around me. I can value and respect them, but they do not own me. I am more than the story that has been woven around me. My past does not have to be my future.

There is a level above this too: in the evolving self, the self-transforming mind in which people can understand and accept and work with their paradoxical nature, recognising and embracing their contradictions.

It is the level of self-authoring and self-transformation at which you can observe yourself as if from above or at a certain distance that you and evaluate what is meaningful and essential to you.

And therein lies an interesting point. According to Kegan, 6% of adults are operating within the frame of an imperial self and 58% within the frame of a socialised person. This means potentially that two-thirds of adults find it difficult, if not impossible, to see themselves clearly. To let go of the wheel and observe who they are and who they might be. It is challenging to change unless you are the captain of your ship; you will wake to be told what is expected of who you are and who you must be. How reliable these numbers are it is difficult to say. Still, if we assume that all of us have some vestiges of the socialised mind inhibiting our ability to see what is there and what we need to do, then surely it is worth working to develop and strengthen this ability.

Transforming the way we see the world

The ability to stand back from being absorbed in our immediate interpretation of events is about 'standing above the action' and seeing yourself as a player in psychological space, an actor involved in a drama or comedy on the stage with other actors. You take the perspective of the director watching how you play your part with others seeking to understand what's going on in the minds of each player and the way that shapes the relationship between them. But lest we take the analogy too far, the director at this stage is just intent on seeing what's happening, noticing things rather than critiquing the actors and preparing 'notes'.

This is an invitation to think about yourself mindfully. Mindfulness is an essential discipline in conscious cognitive reappraisal. As ancient a practice as the development of the *Homo sapiens* brain, its benefits have become very widely understood over the last few decades.

It is possible to imagine this mindfulness as a process or a flow taking you from an old way of looking at the world and you within it to a new way of understanding yourself[4]. It might be useful to see this process as moving through a number of 'zones'.

- **The Mindful Gap** helps us observe the moment without rushing to judgement, creating a crucial pause before reaction.

- **The Mischief Zone** invites playfulness and the questioning of assumptions, breaking us free from rigid patterns of thought.

- **The Creative Space** is where we take ownership, making a deliberate and intentional choice about how to respond.

---

[4] This 'process' goes beyond the strict discipline of mindfulness to include a more deliberately conscious reframing of what is being experienced.

By moving through these zones, we reclaim the ability to control our interpretation of events, staying grounded in what we can change while letting go of what we cannot. This can be applied at in terms of a particular moment or in reflecting on ongoing patterns in our lives.

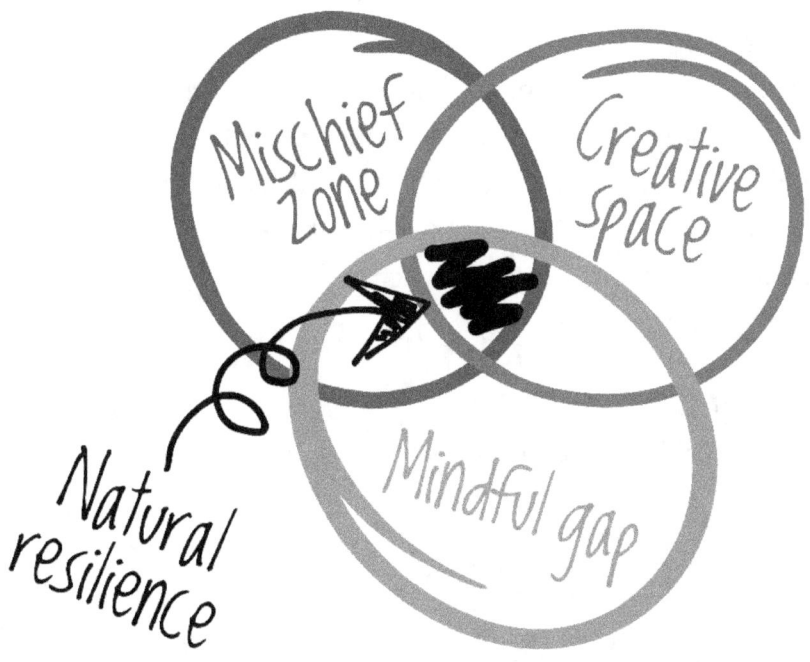

Zone One: The Mindful Gap

Imagine hitting the pause button on reality. In the first zone – the mindful gap – we take a step back and simply observe. No judgement, no reaction, just awareness. What is happening? Who is involved? What is being overlooked?

This practice aligns with mindfulness traditions, which emphasise non-judgemental awareness as a way to create psychological distance from stressors. Neuroscientific research has shown that mindfulness enhances cognitive control and reduces emotional reactivity, making it an essential foundation for cognitive reappraisal.

Let's say you're stuck in a tense conversation with a difficult colleague. Instead of getting sucked into frustration, you step back mentally. You notice their clipped tone, their darting eyes, the way they drum their fingers on the desk. You notice your own body – your shallow breath, the tension in your shoulders. Instead of reacting, you just watch. You don't need to act yet. You are simply present.

This mindful gap opens up space. It gives us a beat before we respond. And in that space, options begin to emerge.

Zone Two: The Mischief Zone

The tendency in shifting out of the mindful gap is to begin to interpret and evaluate. To ask ourselves 'What does what I notice *mean*?', we need to hang on to these hypotheses lightly and instead shift into the mischief zone. This is where we loosen the grip of certainty and embrace playfulness. What if I'm wrong? What if this situation is completely different from how I'm seeing it? What if I turned it on its head? What if that person's tapping finger is not a sign of irritation but listening to an imaginary tune?

This is the perspective of the jester, the trickster, the comic. A difficult moment doesn't have to be an oppressive force: it can be an absurdity waiting to be unmasked. What if the angry colleague isn't really angry but nervous? What if this argument is actually a game, and the rules just need tweaking? And the most disruptive, rebellious questions of all – actually what really matters here?

The mischief zone is crucial because it disrupts rigid thinking. Neuroscience tells us that cognitive flexibility – the ability to shift between different perspectives and problem-solving approaches – is a hallmark of psychological resilience. By introducing humour, absurdity, or counterintuitive thinking, we jolt ourselves out of fixed emotional loops.

In the mischief zone, we might also find room for playful micro-sabotage – not in the destructive sense, but in the art of disrupting expectations. If someone expects you to get defensive, you respond with kindness. If they expect resistance, you offer curiosity. If you expect yourself to spiral into negativity, you surprise yourself with an unexpected thought: *What if this is actually hilarious?*

This step is often overlooked, but it is vital. Without it, cognitive reappraisal risks becoming too rigid or mechanical. The mischief zone keeps things alive, fluid, and adaptable. It allows us to access a broader range of emotional responses, which makes the final lens all the more powerful.

Zone Three: The Creative Space

Finally, we move into the third zone – the creative space. Here, you take everything you've noticed and reframe it into a response that is uniquely yours.

You can't control the behaviour of others, but you *can* control your own story. This is where you ask: What is the most constructive way I can engage? How can I act with intention rather than impulse? What is within my power to change?

The creative zone is where we translate insight into action. This might mean adopting a Stoic approach, focusing only on what is within our control and letting go of the rest. The Stoics believed that true freedom comes from governing our own reactions rather than trying to bend the world to our will. This idea is deeply empowering – we move from feeling like victims of circumstance to architects of our own responses.

It might mean crafting a response that aligns with our values rather than our immediate emotions. It could involve seeing an obstacle as an opportunity or turning a challenge into a personal experiment.

Maybe the creative response is humour. Maybe it's disengagement. Maybe it's a calm, clear statement of your boundaries. Maybe it's choosing to reframe a setback as an opportunity. Whatever the response, it is yours: not dictated by circumstances but crafted by your own agency.

Creating this space in our thought and emotions unlocks the door to the potential we have to access out natural resilience and out the rich potential of our wholeself.

Sometimes it can be as simple as asking yourself some questions.

Mindful Gap: 'Why am I unhappy? Thinking about it, I am fed up with work but feel I need the money. I have so many responsibilities? I always seem to think like this. I am unhappy, it must be my job. I think about leaving and then I think about the responsibilities I have for my family and feel it would be a disaster if I left, so I should stick with my job.'

Mischief Zone: 'So I am totally dependent on this job to survive? Yes. So, it will last forever and I am safe? Well actually they made a lot of people redundant last year, who knows what will happen. But I am totally dependent on this job? Well not totally dependent, my partner has just been promoted! What might I do if I let go of this assumption that I need to work here?'

Creative Space: 'I could spend more time with my family as I don't like these shifts where I never see the kids. I could set myself up as gardener, something I love doing. I love being outdoors and I know that I am good at it. Alternatively, I could stay if I found a way of enjoying my job more. I mean my job isn't going to change, but if I think about it, I really enjoy working with the other guys – perhaps I should focus more on that and the mentoring I am doing for apprentices.'

Of course, this is a simplistic example but, in the example, the actual situation is not necessarily changing; but the way that it is being perceived is.

This ability to establish control on how we see a situation gives us the real power to change our story, by focusing on these elements of our lives that point us towards a richer and more complete experience.

Chapter 8: The Rewilded Self

How do you mobilise all these gifts you have been given: your natural resilience, your psychodiversity, your ability to reflect and understand who you are? How do you turn your possibility to actuality? The path to restoration might begin just outside your window.

I live in a little house on the edge of a small, modern estate. The estate has been thoughtfully laid out with areas of grass with play areas for young children. It is surrounded on all sides by older houses and roads. In the background you can always hear the low, steady thrum of the A50 trunk road. It is without doubt suburban, cultivated and domesticated. Residents pay a small fee each year for common areas of grass to be mown, the weeds to be beaten back, things to be kept ordered and regulated.

But from the window of my study, I can see a big old oak tree and behind that a copse of trees. A useful path runs through it to the local pub. This small piece of woodland, a few hundred metres long and 40 metres wide, is a minor miracle. In it you will find old yew trees, sycamores, fledgling elm, holly, and hawthorn. Despite the yew trees, whose fallen needles carpet the ground, bluebells and blackberry push through. It is often alive with the sound of rooks, blackbirds, wood pigeons, jackdaws, and robins. My neighbour Greg, who keeps his eye on such things, tells me that sparrowhawks have nested in the trees, hedgehogs abide and a one-eyed rat comes to call. He also told me that muntjac deer have been spotted.

The older trees here are probably related to other trees in the village. Forested land once more-or-less-continuously stretched from here to Sherwood Forest, then 30 miles away in Nottinghamshire. In the village church yard is an ancient yew tree, held up with chains and iron poles. It is over 1,400 years old, 500 years older than the church itself, which has seen but 950 years. Robin Hood was said to be married under it to the fair Clorinda (Maid Marian).

If we want a model for effective resilience, we should look no further than nature itself. If we want to understand how to take advantage of our psychodiversity and natural resilience perhaps the lessons lie not just in exposure to nature itself but the way that nature as an 'ecosystem' works.

One of the most heartening concepts to have emerged in the last few years is the notion of rewilding. Actually, it is more than heartening. When I first started to read about it, I felt I had come across something deeply profound, moving, and optimistic. I was literally moved to tears as the implications of it sunk in. Rewilding shows the incredible innate ability of an ecosystem to repair and *heal itself, if it is left alone.* When it is given the 'space' to recover and renew.

There is a rapidly growing body of evidence of the power of this. Rewilding isn't about returning nature to some imagined, untouched past. It's about restoring the conditions under which a natural system can regenerate, adapt, and evolve *on its own terms.* In this view, nature is not something to be repaired, but something capable of repairing itself, if given the right space and diversity to do so. Rewilding can be contrasted with conservation. Conservation is about returning an environment to some arbitrary earlier state by actively managing that environment with a high level of involvement and control. In many ways that environment remains dependent on external oversight.

Famous examples of rewilding include the pioneering work of Isabella Tree and Charlie Burrell on the Knepp estate in West Sussex, England. Turning their land over to be governed by rewilding principles has resulted in dramatic improvements in the numbers, variety and health of species of flora and fauna: 150 bird species have been recorded on the estate since the rewilding began with several species such as the nightingale increasing significantly, from just a handful to over 100 breeding pairs. The number of butterfly species grew from 20 to 40. The number of plant species grew from 35 to 90. One of the most important improvements was in soil quality, where soil organic carbon levels increased by an average of 25%, something incredibly important in terms of countering global warming.

Similarly, in Ireland the death-metal loving, ponytailed Randall Plunkett, also known as Lord Dunsany, found that when he moved a large part of his estate over to rewilding the whole place started to regenerate. Where there were three types of grass there are now 23. Oak, ash, beach, Scots pine and black poplar saplings started growing, not because he had planted them, but because the seeds had been blown in or brought in by birds.

Beyond the increase in numbers of species something else starts to occur. Something remarkable happens when you enable rewilding: *emergence.*

Emergence describes the way in which new, often unpredictable forms and behaviours arise from interactions within complex systems and the establishment of interdependence. These patterns can't be understood by analysing the parts in isolation – they appear only in the whole. There is a kind of self-management going on within the ecosystem: a murmuration of starlings, the structure of a beehive, or the regeneration of a clear-cut forest all reveal how life can self-organise into coherence without a central plan.

The Rewilded Self

An environment is one thing, human mental life is another, you might argue. What can one tell us about the other? Perhaps one can stand as a model for another.

Good old Aristotle, amongst others, saw the power of analogical reasoning, drawing parallels between two domains or concepts that may seem unrelated at first to understand and explain one of them better. There are lessons and insights that can be drawn from understanding what we know about ecological systems that can illuminate how we understand our inner life.

You are, *your wholeself is*, in short, a *psychological ecosystem* – your thoughts, emotions, motivations, relationships, and bodily states exist as a complexity of oppositional parts, with high levels of interconnectedness and emergent phenomena, given the mental space discussed in the previous chapter. Within it, things like creativity, healing, joy, and insight are not manufactured on command. They *emerge* from the dynamic interplay of your inner and outer life.

And so, just as environmental ecosystems can be rewilded, perhaps we can begin to psychologically rewild, creating the conditions in which natural resilience and potential can *emerge from within*.

Rewilding an ecosystem seems to centre around a limited number of principles:

- encourage diversity
- enable natural processes
- establish keystone species
- moderate external control
- build corridors and connections

So how might these relate to our ability to ourselves to write a new story which makes us less helpless, more engaged with the possibility of ourselves?

Encourage diversity

In ecology, diversity is not just aesthetic – it's functional. In the Oostvaardersplassen nature reserve in the Netherlands, rewilding efforts reintroduced a wide mix of grazing species. The result was not chaos, but the re-emergence of layered plant and animal communities that hadn't existed there for centuries. Biodiversity became the engine of renewal.

The great ecologist David Tilman showed that the greater the diversity that occurred within a system, the more robust and resilient that system was. Systems with low diversity are more vulnerable and more dependent upon outside support.

The same principle applies internally. As we have seen, it is about not being too narrow in your understanding of yourself, in the story you are creating about who you are. Psychological resilience depends on psychodiversity – inhabiting your wholeself in all its contradictory and dynamic potential.

Abundance, in this light, is not a surplus of positivity or calm. It is *the fullness of our inner ecosystem* – the ability to hold joy and grief, ambition and rest, structure and spontaneity. Just as a forest thrives through layered interdependence, the psyche thrives when its contradictions are allowed to coexist. As with the case of my late father, we are not one thing or another: we are one thing *and* another. Celebrate and honour *all* that you are: don't overlook parts of yourself because they do not seem valued by others, or don't seem to 'fit in' with the narrative that has woven itself around you. Be your wholeself.

Enable Natural Processes

Rewilded ecosystems depend on the return of natural processes: letting seed dispersal happen, decomposition of flora and fauna, natural fires, increases in diversity and soil regeneration profoundly impact the health of that ecosystem. So too can reintroducing native species. In the UK reintroducing beavers has had transformative effects. By building dams, they restore natural water flow, increase biodiversity, and reduce downstream flooding – all by simply doing what they are biologically designed to do.

Similarly, the human system begins to rebalance when we *restore basic psychological and physiological processes*: sleep, rest, exploration, movement, connection, creation and learning. These are not indulgences; they are foundational.

A burned-out executive who reintroduces daily walking and unstructured reading time may find that the pressure to 'solve' a problem gives way to something better: a *sense of perspective*, a loosening, and eventually, a creative or emotional breakthrough. These breakthroughs are often *emergent phenomena* – they arise from a system that has been gently returned to its natural rhythm.

People often report that real shifts occur only when they stop trying so hard – whether through mindfulness, therapy, movement, or simply permission to feel, the system begins to breathe again. And in that breath, new responses, insights, and emotional states can emerge without being forced.

Abundance here is not in productivity, but in *possibility* – the capacity of the psyche to surprise us with what it can reorganise, reinterpret, and resolve on its own.

Establish keystone species: risk matters

In virtually any ecosystem there are two sorts of keystone species: landscape architects and apex predators. Together they disproportionally shape the environment in which they exist. Landscape architects are often large herbivores like elephants or cattle, or in the past, aurochs and mammoths. Their grazing behaviour dramatically impacts a landscape as does the rooting, digging and building activities of animals such as wild boar and beavers. The psychological equivalent would be in our need to learn from others, particular new ideas which shape the psychological world in which you exist.

Reintroducing apex predators into the environment is often controversial, establishing a 'tropic cascade' in which a threat of becoming something's lunch really shapes behaviour.

I once went to a safari park in South Africa. A large fence ran down the middle of the park. In one half, a full range of animals were allowed to roam. In the other half were the same animals minus the lions and the cheetah. The two halves gave very different visitor experiences. In the non-predator half, the animals were lounging around, taking in the sun, digesting lunch, perhaps contemplating a little swim in the creek. In the predator half the atmosphere was altogether vigilant. If you saw an animal, it was a more fleeting glimpse, you had to look harder and wait longer. From a visitor point of view, of course, the former is more immediately impactful, but I would argue that the kudu, warthog, wildebeest and zebra were behaving more naturally when threatened with the presence of a lion or a cheetah. Risk seems to be an essential functioning of an ecosystem. If it is removed the system quite quickly starts to degrade. A good example of this is the exploding deer population in Scotland where the absence of apex predators such as lynx and wolves has meant that large numbers of deer and causing great damage to the environment and reducing the vitality of the ecosystem in which they live.

In the US, the reintroduction of wolves into Yellowstone National Park is one of the most cited successes of rewilding. These apex predators reshaped the ecosystem – not just by culling deer, but by triggering changes in animal behaviour, vegetation, and even river structure. One reintroduced element had *ripple effects across the entire system.*

In the psychological landscape, *risk* plays a similarly catalytic role. When we step into discomfort – whether by expressing something vulnerable, starting a creative project, or confronting a limiting belief – we destabilise the known, we recognise the uncertainty, we create a learning opportunity. That moment of disequilibrium invites new states and ideas to surface: courage, playfulness, rebellion, certainly creativity even compassion for ourselves. This is a better calibration of ways to deal with the risks inherent in an Impossible World. Risk is inevitable; how we deal with it is a choice.

Minimise external control

In conservation, heavy-handed management often backfires. The suppression of fire in certain US forests, for example, led to denser undergrowth and more devastating wildfires. Only by allowing natural burn cycles to resume could the ecosystem regain its balance. Famously, another example of this over control was the introduction of cane toads in the 1930s into Australia from Hawaii. The idea was that the toads would eat beetles that were damaging the sugar cane crops. The toads, however, really liked Australia and bred with enthusiasm, becoming quickly an out-of-control invasive pest, their toxins leading to rapid decline in a number of native species and widespread disruption of local ecosystems. Conservation is an outside-in strategy seeking to manage an ecosystem back to arbitrarily defined 'better state'.

Psychologically, the same holds true. The master-servant relationship is based on the fact that someone else knows best. When faced with adversity, our first instinct may be to seek help. We may expect that someone somewhere 'knows' what to do and will save us. That someone may be the government, our doctor, our boss, our partner, an expert somewhere. All together, they make up that strange, elusive group of people called the 'They.' You hear about them all the time. In conversations, in the newspaper, in social media: 'They think... They suggest... They have discovered...'

'They' often haven't a clue!

A few years ago, I set out to walk through the forests of Tennessee and North Carolina along the rarely visited Benton Mackay Trail. Before I left, everyone (well, many people), asked not about my goals: to explore the land of the Cherokee nation; to experience what it means truly to carry my means of survival through the wilderness; to search out in my little way the soul of America. No, it was to talk about bears! Black bears, how dangerous they were, how unpredictable, how very unafraid of humans they have become, how fortunate I was that there were only black bears when there might have been grizzlies. People who had never strayed beyond seeing a glass-eyed bear on the edge of their pillow earnestly told me I should know that grizzlies were much, much worse.

And then came the stream of advice. Stand your ground and look big. Shout. Speak quietly but firmly. Make sure you are not between a mother bear and her cubs. Shoot them. Hang your food bag high up the tree so they can't climb up and get it. Wear different clothes to sleep in than you have cooked in. Leave the latter at least 100 metres away from wherever you are sleeping. Bears, it seems, have a surprising interest in personal hygiene, and your toothbrush and toothpaste, plus any soaps and wet wipes, should be hung in the tree with the food as well.

The best and most cynical advice was not to mess around and run like hell.

And then, with the theatrical pause:

> 'Bears can run at 30 miles-an-hour so you won't escape, but at least you'll feel you're doing something useful before it grabs you and tears you to pieces.'

Towards the departure date, the advice by text, email, and Facebook messages steadily mounted, along with more suggestions, well-wishes and prayers. Surely, I thought, I can't have that many friends who have come across bears or researched their behaviour and psychology. Two nights before I left, I was playing a gig. When introducing a new song I had written about America, I good-naturedly grumbled about this stream of expertise and joked, 'Please! No more advice about bears!'

Blow me, at the interval, someone came up to me and said:

> 'I know you said you had had quite a lot of advice about bears…'

> 'No,' I replied. 'I'd had *too much* advice about bears and couldn't take any more.'

> 'Well anyway,' he went on, 'a good idea I heard was to…'

Now, the problem often is that every crisis, personal or global, is unique, and 'they' too often don't trouble themselves to understand the situation or the context before launching into a stream of advice and instruction.

Rewilding is much more an inside-out strategy, in which we take responsibility for our own worlds. Sure, advice is useful but it is our responsibility to seek it and evaluate it. And from an inside-out point of view, we should also be mindful of those expectations and control instructions we have probably unknowingly internalised – all those *shoulds*, *oughts* and *musts* that have taken us hostage. In rewilding ourselves, we are taking back control of who we are to enable our resourcefulness to flourish.

Create Corridors and Connections

In nature, wildlife corridors are essential. In Europe, rewilding projects link fragmented habitats, allowing wolves, bears, and lynx to roam and breed. Connectivity leads to genetic resilience, species mixing, and wider ecosystem health.

Our psychological ecosystems are also fragmented – often by trauma, isolation, cultural conditioning, or busyness. Creating corridors between our inner states (body and mind, past and present, self and other) and between ourselves and others reactivates the system's *inherent interdependence*. Increasingly as tribal structures and communities breakdown we live lonely, disconnected lives. An essential part of our wellbeing is the relationships we have with others.

One of the most beautiful feelings we can experience is that of rapport. That deep connection when two minds seem to meld together. The deep presence of another enables co-regulation – the way one nervous system calms in the presence of another is not just emotional hygiene. It is a form of *interpersonal biodiversity*: two complex systems meeting and, in their interaction, generating something new. Obviously, this is something we hope to find with our partners, but it is also the joy in working in a team, playing with like-minded musicians, dancing with a partner. Not surprisingly, this is a summoning of our natural resilience.

The Rewilded Self

There are many lessons we can learn from nature and we will return to some of them again but to summarise for now, the ideas of rewilding *make room for us to recover ourselves to liberate our 'wholeself'*. Rewilding opens up system's ability to change, renew, and respond. And often, what arises from this process is not what we expected, but something richer.

This is the nature of emergence and the liberation of our natural resourcefulness. Our rewilded life won't be one of neat solutions, but of new patterns. It offers not just recovery, but *transformation* – that beautiful arc of recovery we saw in a distressed child, not to calm passivity but to active engagement. And in doing so, it leads us to the deepest form of abundance, not the abundance of accumulation or certainty, but of *possibility*, *relationship*, and *surprising aliveness*. Of thriving, so much more than just surviving.

Just as rewilded landscapes become more complex, more interconnected, and more alive, so too can our inner worlds – when we stop trying to force them and begin to trust the system within.

Lessons for the Rewilded Self

- Be your 'wholeself' – explore all that you might be

- Nurture the healer within – sleep, food, fitness, reflection, and learning

- Embrace uncertainty – accept risk as a condition for flourishing

- Be the author of your own story – take control of your narrative

- Connect with others – emotionally and spiritually

Part Three: Five Practices for a Wholehearted Life

Chapter 9: Readiness

If this were a proper 'How to' book, I would be inviting you to set a number of personal development goals to develop your natural resilience and your rewilded self, in order to create a fabulous new you! But in an uncertain Impossible World that may not be a viable option, where things are so uncertain and therefore unpredictable.

Undoubtedly goals are useful, and we need them when we need to focus, but surviving and thriving in an Impossible World means that overfocus can be a danger. It can make us blind to the situation we are in and how we might be responding to it. Grimly focused on a specific result, we do not see the world changing so that the goal becomes impossible or redundant.

You might be the captain of your ship, but you are not a ferry sailing towards a fixed destination. You are putting to sea to explore and discover. We may have an overall sense of what we would like to find, but the how, where and when of that we must allow to evolve and change.

We need to be ready for the unexpected and the sudden 'offer' of opportunity which we choose or ignore. Like Paul McCartney meeting John Lennon for the first time at a church fete where Lennon's band was performing. What would have happened if McCartney had decided that day not to go? And what if he hadn't already spent hours learning the guitar to a level such that when they met, Lennon could see a gifted musician and the spark was struck.

Surviving and Thriving in an Impossible World depends upon being open and ready for the offer that the moment affords, as much as upon the pursuit of temporary goals. It is about being ready for serendipity. In the previous chapter, I wrote about how the positive and unexpected can emerge from a healthy ecosystem, and so too in a psychological ecosystem. This *emergence from within* opens the door to serendipity.

Serendipity is a magic word. It was first coined by Horace Walpole in *The Three Princes of Serendip*, who were 'always making discoveries, by accident and sagacity, of things they were not in the quest of.' Could these 'happy accidents' occur as internal emergent phenomena bump into the emergent opportunities of the systems in which we operate?

So much of the truth of our world is an unexpected discovery: from the microwave oven invented by a man whose radar equipment melted the candy in his pockets; to the popsicle, when an 11-year-old accidentally left a mix of water and soda powder outside to freeze. It is a concept that intrigues scientists and technologists who recognise that it is the unforeseen and unplanned that often provide the breakthrough insight.

In a blog in *Scientific American*[5], Karla Starr explores how scientific discovery is often a 'happy accident'. Laboratories that have a relentless focus in testing and noticing nothing but the hypothesis may be efficient, but 'it also guarantees that a lab will never make a truly remarkable or unexpected discovery.'

Karla Starr highlights the fact that internet users 'engaged in casual browsing may be the most receptive to information that is just outside their specific goals.' So many breakthroughs come from the unexpected result being *noticed*. The most famous may be Penicillin; but remember, Viagra was intended to be a treatment for high blood pressure and angina.

Going back to Horace Walpole's original formula, it is not just accidents you need for serendipity but 'sagacity.' Sagacity is the ability to see the opportunity and to realise its potential. In other words, it requires the freedom to be present and notice

---

[5] *How to Find What You Are Not Looking For*, Scientific American, September 2012

things at the edge of your perception and the freedom to be inconsistent and look at something in a new way.

I think the power of serendipity has been ongoing throughout my life and I have taken much joy and success from its elusive promise. From the job that changed my life, readvertised as a filler in the *Guardian* on April Fools' Day, through to discovering, in amongst a great random pile of papers that I put in my bag as I left one job, a brief account of the work of Michael Apter, my life has been changed by the unlooked-for. That brief article, grasped at the last minute as I cleared my desk, led me to help create new models of work, analytic tools, and an international network of colleagues.

One of the most wonderful examples of the transformational qualities of serendipity is a trip I made on foot from the top of the Atlas Mountains along the old camel routes, across the anti-Atlas Mountains and into the desert, a journey of just over 500km. The original reasons for this trip were a bit fuzzy. A few before me have stood on the top of Mount Toubkal and gazed eastwards imagining what it would be like to walk from there to the Sahara Desert. And that simple 'because it's there' notion seemed to attract all sorts of opportunities and mysteries. I found I was following the never completed journey of the writer Gavin Maxwell, someone who I had admired since boyhood. Someone mentioned I might come across a lost tribe of dwarves written about by an eccentric but very determined Canadian lawyer in the 19th century. I discovered that without design the route would take us through the resting place of the old Krupp cannon given to the local Berber warlord by the Sultan of Morocco, a gift which irrevocably changed the history of that country. And most moving of all, as the theme of so much of my work is 'freedom' in all its resonances, I discovered the Berber world for themselves is *Imazighen*, which means freemen.

Oh, and I may have found the 'lost tribe'.

So, by all means have goals – but set them in the more inclusive context of your readiness and sagacity to seize the opportunities that serendipitously flow your way, enabling you to inhabit your 'wholeself'.

Ready for Serendipity

In 2013, I wrote a book called *A Little Nostalgia for Freedom*. This was an idiosyncratic exploration of a question that had haunted me from childhood.

Why is it that we find it so hard to do in life the things we really want to? And, more importantly, what might we do about it?

These two questions have, over the years, morphed into the more complex agenda of a deeper understanding of a relationship that we might have with the world and ourselves, an agenda that has been explored in this book. But the practical answers to the question seem to illuminate a personal path you might take too.

I hope I travel with the wisdom of all the articles, research, and experiments I have studied as a psychologist – but I hold them lightly, for the experience of the road is a powerful critic of abstract ideas, as well as the conjurer of new ones. In *A Little Nostalgia for Freedom,* I went looking for the world of pirates, explorers, troubadours and adventurers in Salé, Morocco, the Sahara Desert, Kowloon, London, and New York, which taught me much about the longing for another life so many of us have. It also raised the question: what do we do when we need the freedom to do the things really want to do?

In the book I proposed five practices[6] gathered like ancient tools from my travels which enable you to be both more deeply of aware of the world and yourself but also able to respond to this in a resourceful way. They offer the chance to rewrite your life. They cover how to build the conditions for the full, abundant and less-helpless life explored in Part Two. They are the practices for a life that might be lived wholeheartedly.

In them, you will find ways to loosen the bonds of your servant mindset in which you have grown and to become less afraid of fear. You will find ways to gain the natural resilience you were born with, the psychodiversity that is your essential being, the strength to stand back and see what is really going on, and the opportunity to rewild yourself. To open yourself up to the

---

[6] Which I called at the time 'Rules of the Road'.

universal law of happy accidents. You could say that if you follow these practices, you will develop a readiness to flourish in an Impossible World.

The rules are:

- **Be Wild** – work to see what is really there within and without you

- **Be Strong** – discover and build the strengths through which you can embrace uncertainty

- **Be Experimental** – confront life, not as a grand strategic plan executed over a number of years, but as a series of experiments through which you can learn what works for you by engaging your wholeself

- **Travel with Companions** – build relationships with those who will love you enough to tell you the truth and sacrifice themselves, if needed, in that spirit

- **Take the First Step** – do not procrastinate. Even if you just take a small step, start today on the road that calls you

Chapter 10: Be Wild

Be connected to the moment, observing what is really happening, letting go of all the 'filters' to your attention, like your servant mindset, your chains to the past and the future, the assumptions that dictate your life. Open yourself to the possibility and potential of the world and yourself. Write a new story.

I've heard somewhere that the aborigines of Australia say you are never truly in the wild until you're four days in; four days into the forest; four days into the desert. Now, four days is a literal amount of time, which I have noticed to be very, very accurate. Four days into hiking on the Benton MacKaye Trail, four days out into the Atlas Mountains, four days on a yacht on the Croatian coast – and your head is in a very different place.

Weary and filthy after five days walking through the steaming forests of Appalachia I noted in a journal:

One glorious lunch, I sat on the banks of the broad Ocoee River under a tree. I lay in an eddying pool shaped by spring waters and let the river run over me. I felt I was not just in the wild, but of it. I realised over the days since we had left Atlanta, and particularly since Everett had dropped us by the road, it was more than the unnecessary contents of my backpack I had put down. It was the clutter of life.

It is that sweet moment when you find yourself no longer looking into a landscape but out from it.

Four Days In

'Four days in' is a practical recipe for a powerful state of mind. I am not saying you should regularly go and spend four days in the wilderness, although I miss it when I don't! But knowing deeply and intimately this sense of being present and uncluttered in your thinking and observation is a powerful point of reference to how much progress you are making to Being Wild. When people talk about taking 'time out' they may mean they are taking a rest only to resume the same old 'same old' again. Wildness is the ability to stand back *at any time* and evaluate what is going on and what matters.

Being wild is the first step to liberation. It is about learning to see more of what is there and the possibility of what is there both within and without ourselves. In doing this, you are reclaiming the freedom to be present. You are reawakening your awareness of the potential in yourself and in the world. It is about being able to break out of the hostage servant mindset.

And in that, it is a revolutionary act, perhaps the most fundamental revolutionary act. It is not to accept the given in what we see, we feel, we do, we expect.

It is not about replacing one fixed mindset with another. It is about being able to rotate our perspectives on what is happening to us and around us to take multiple views of a situation. I think this is a greater ability for leaders and others than raw intelligence. In fact, it is clearly the case as I look out at the world that many leaders can be quite clever but find being wild impossible.

If we look at our lives, this ability to stand back from ourselves and realise what is happening to us and what is happening in the system around us is an important and necessary first step to increasing our resourcefulness, our adaptability, and the likelihood that we will flourish. It requires the level of adult maturity we discussed earlier. Being wild develops self-awareness. Ironically, it also frees you from self-consciousness. For self-consciousness is the internalised judgement by others that inhibits so many of us. Being self-conscious is when you make a negative judgement about yourself, and it belongs to an over-shaped mind.

So being wild begins by undoing or at least breaking up a little the framework of expectations we have learned and developed through our childhoods into adulthood and work and the culture into which we are born. Daniel Kahneman, years ago, pointed out how our brain must develop heuristics and biases, mental models to deal with the world on a fast-moving basis. Necessarily, these mental models include stereotypes, wrongful assumptions, simplifications, and abstractions. In an Impossible World, we need to put these assumptions on trial for their lives. The killer question being 'Do they serve?'

Imagining wild

When I think of being wild, I like to think of images. I think of the owl in the tree observing, moving his head, gauging an opportunity in front of him, or the lion watching the herd of zebra. Or a golfer, sizing up a putt from several angles. Or the rugby player kicking for the posts as the crowd quietens and murmurs, judging the angle, the distance, the wind, and the beating of his heart.

Each one of these pays 100% attention to the here and now and the reality they are living in. I think of the way a young child looks at the world, totally absorbed in it. The first pure quality, therefore, of wildness is the ability to pay full attention to what is going on.

And, in this, being wild, is also about creating a sense of distance from yourself to be able to observe yourself within that situation in a kind of engaging disengagement. This allows you to examine, 'How am I feeling of the moment? What thoughts am I having? What am I expecting? Where is this situation with me in it going?'

Being wild brings your whole life to the present – the only moment you can directly shape. You are opening yourself to what the situation affords rather than prejudging and trying to control some future version of it. I remember listening to the poet David Whyte. In between reciting two of his poems, he was talking about how things happen and must happen. 'The farmer can't hurry the harvest,' he said. 'He can only be strong and ready for it when it arrives.'

Can you realistically live your whole life like this? Open to the possibility of the present, letting life unfold to take you where it will rather than chasing the future? Perhaps for most people, this would be too much. But not for everyone. Meet Bean're.

Bean're

It was hot, incredibly hot, and humid, and my backpack had rubbed bits of my skin red raw, and my feet were battered and sore. After six days on the trail, I was done in. I paused to rest awhile in a little place called Reliance near the Hiwassee River, more particularly in the Webb Brothers Gas Station and Store, which had thoughtfully provided a big old leather armchair for me to sit in. I must have fallen asleep, for when I awoke, a tall fellow was standing by the counter talking to Eve, the shop manager. He was a tall, middle-aged man, not too many pounds on him, wearing cowboy boots, beat-up jeans, and an old sun-bleached shirt with a red bandanna around his neck. He had long greying hair in a ponytail, a goatee beard, and a smiling face that had seen much wind and sun.

'I have a good life,' he was saying. 'Just me and the bike. There's not much work in these parts, so I don't hang around looking for it. I rode up the coast on a minibike last year. I think it might be in some sort of record book.'

Eve smiled and handed him his change but said nothing. With a wave to Eve and a 'howdy' at me, he turned and strode out, kicked his Harley into life, and rode out of Reliance. I dozed off again. When I got back to England, I thought a lot about motorbikes and America and the romance of the live-fast, die-young dream. Bikes and freedom go hand in hand in the American myth. They seemed to represent some elemental throwback to the idea of 'escape' that brought so many people from the narrow, circumscribed lives of Europe and elsewhere.

I started working on a new song, 'The Ballad of the Dragon's Tail,' about this emblematic romance. I built the song around the character I had seen at the store back in Reliance. On a whim one night, after finishing and recording the song, I searched on the internet for 'world record minibike journey,' and there he was: 'Bean're, one of the last American nomads.' An ex-marine who doesn't drink or do drugs, he hit the road years ago on his trusty old Harley. Like an excellent eastern guru, albeit one who tends to sport a long ponytail and a top hat, he sees possessions as a form of imprisonment: no house, no regular employment just the open road, and an international network of goodwill. Not surprisingly, in certain circles, he has near-legendary status. His website details his adventures and calls him the 'Mayor of Fun' and is adorned with photos of him out on the road: riding his Harley standing up and hanging out in the wilderness. On the cover of the book he later sent me – inscribed from the 'Motorcycle Nomad to the Vagabond Philosopher' – it shows a 'pulp fiction' illustration of him riding an old bike away from a pursuing posse with a western steam train running alongside.

How would it be to let the world come to you more often, rather than spending your days in relentless pursuit of it?

Maybe this would be too much for most people. But I have an increasing number of friends who have radically changed their perspective on life and freed themselves from a neurotic fixation with the future. They are building their faith in their resourcefulness.

Sure, set goals, they can help us move forward but be prepared to discard them quickly if they no longer work.

Adventures and Investigations

These '**Adventures and Investigations**' are strategies, lights-on-the-horizon stories, and ideas through which you can liberate yourself by crafting your life to become more resourceful, more open to the unfolding possibility of yourself. These thoughts reflect a lifetime of practice in all aspects of my vagabond life.

Becoming wild means disconnecting from the noise in your head and the voices of others and reconnecting with the world you are in and the potential you have.

All of three of the suggestions below are to some extent ways to be mindful.

To **Be Wild** consider, perhaps, to:

- Go Sauntering
- Go and Get Lost
- Go Outdoors

Go Sauntering

We are walking animals. Our ancestors walked every day. They walked from food source to food source. They walked from hut to field. They walked to escape and to conquer. Our bodies are designed for it. Our babies are born helpless so that women can keep walking, the trade-off between hip size for locomotion and baby weight.

Walking has the deepest and most profound physiological impact upon us, and it has been shown to increase working memory, creative thinking, and problem-solving. And as importantly, as shown by Robert Thayer of California State University, to impact positively upon self-esteem, happiness, energy levels, and reduce tension. Walking is an opportunity to literally step outside to engage with the world in new ways.

It is a place where the background noise of life has disappeared, when the memories come to you about yourself and what's happened, when you look on and observe, the emotional content turned down a little. Problems are solved as you walk through the trail by the river and along the road. Perspective is gained. It is the single most excellent psychological therapy I have ever come across. Walking reconnects us in the words of *Psychology Today* to the 'self-generative imaginative capacities of ourselves and disconnects us from the chronic bombardment of prefabricated imagery.'

A note from a journal entry of mine four days in, on a trek through the Atlas Mountains with my friend 'Brahim:

> *For a few days, we crisscrossed the passes and valleys of the region, camping out in deserted valleys and the crest of mountain passes. I had worried about my fitness, but apart from a mild headache that disappeared by day two, I felt fine.*
>
> *I had come on this trip from a stressful and complex existence and noticed I was becoming increasingly relaxed. My life at that time was an impossible intersection of competing goals and demands. Dealing with them here was impossible, and they quickly faded to a vague zero. Travelling on foot, I noticed, has a simplifying effect. When the challenge in front of you is a steep 500m ascent and a blistering hot day, then more intangible concerns and worries tend to be in full retreat. The effect was amazingly liberating. When daily life becomes the pursuit of a limited number of clear, simple tasks, then I could see how the past, present, and future rebalance themselves. I could also see how it was possible to pursue more audaciously a dream of the life you wanted to live when you were not dragging around a sack full of competing goals.*
>
> *I mused on the causes of my newfound state of mind. At walking, pace life grows in intensity and richness. You notice things or see them more thoroughly. For instance,*

> take the mud. The mud of Morocco is not brown, at least not in the Atlas Mountains. In the High Atlas Mountains, it is cinnamon, ochre, olive, purple, khaki, red as rust, even blue as eggshells. Yet until yesterday, I would have called it brown. I remembered some psychological research that showed that walking improved our ability to perceive things and discriminate in detail. Was it fanciful, I wondered, to imagine that it also makes social perception more discriminatory, helping us to see what is important.

I should be clear here what I mean by walking. I have friends who are seriously good hikers: taking ultra-long-distance treks is what they love. Their days are marked by mileages or kilometres to be achieved. I honour them for their skill, their toughness, and their dedication. I also know I drive them mad.

For mostly, I want to *saunter*. I am totally with the great writer Henry David Thoreau who wondered if sauntering was derived from a medieval conman called the 'Sainte-Terrer'. This was someone who begged from alms to go to the holy land with no intention of getting there. Or perhaps it came from 'sans terre', without land or home. Either way, to such walkers, destination is of little importance. Walking to be wild needs to be entirely undertaken for its own sake. And at a particular pace.

Research into the neuropsychology of walking showed that the most significant positive impacts were in light to moderate paces, a moderate pace being a mile in 15 to 20 minutes. (1km in 9½ to 12½ mins). Light to medium paces have positive impacts on psychological well-being, including lowering depression and reducing pain severity. Quite marvellously, these positive effects were not found at greater speed.

Go and get lost

Enabling yourself to have the capacity for a more liberated response to it is going to be at the heart of your well-being. You might also need to embrace the sense of being lost reasonably regularly!

Being lost is about not knowing where you are and not knowing where to go next. Or both. Being lost is not knowing what is essential, what matters, what is expected. It is when 'they are not around to help. It is not knowing what a reasonable goal might be.

This can be disturbing.

Our childhood fears of wolves in the wood, sleeping dragons, or being alone in the wilderness make being lost troubling. It brings out the vulnerable boy or girl within us, instinctively reaching up an arm to take a parent's hand.

But being lost is also a problem to solve, a land to be discovered, the key to the prison cell, the place you finally meet yourself.

To be afraid of getting lost is to be afraid of living.

I have had the immense privilege of being remarkably lost in the Atlas Mountains, the Sahara Desert, Tsim Tsa Chui in Kowloon, New Mexico, the back streets of Athens, Germany (where I accidentally ended up in Poland), and Nashville – nobody told me there were two Nashvilles in the US.

I have also been more psychologically lost – when I left University without a clue of what to do with my life. When, as a teacher, I ran out of the love for the job, When I was recruited to a role in an organisation which the Finance Director informed me on day one didn't exist and hadn't been agreed. Or when as above, my business collapsed around my ears. All of which unexpectedly led me to quite wonderful discoveries.

As you enter the 'borderlands' between the assumptions and expectations of the old world and the potential of a place where nothing makes sense, a kind of psychological wilderness, embracing the feeling of being lost and then liberating yourself, may turn out to be one of the significant challenges of your life.

I mean this literally and figuratively. Getting lost awakens you more than anything else to the situation you are in and the way you are dealing with it – that feeling of being out of your depth, disoriented and on your own. The first thing you meet when you get lost is yourself: your emotions, your abilities, or lack of them, your judgements about the situation.

I travel chaotically. The secrets of the competent wanderer are lost on me. Considering the farrago of misunderstood directions, impossible transport connections, and incipient disaster I bring to the endeavour, the fact that I invariably get to my destination is most often due to the kindness of strangers rather than navigational talent.

I speak, therefore, as one who knows.

Choosing to be lost is not so hard. It is letting a chance rather than map guide your way. It is about doing something unfamiliar to you. It is doing something you have perhaps dismissed, something you were not capable of or of which not all others would approve. It is about positioning yourself nearer to the Weird World than The Village.

Getting lost is about putting yourself undoubtedly in your discomfort zone!

The great joy about getting properly lost is you never quite get home again. For the act of adapting to the challenge changes you forever.

Think of your first day at school or in a new job. How lost were you? But you could not find your way back to where you were even if you wanted to.

Go Outdoors

If walking and getting lost seem, at this moment, too big a step, start close in. Simply go outside, at least as far as nature resides. At your core, you are deeply wired for the natural world. This is the essence of *biophilia* – the innate human tendency to seek connection with nature and other forms of life. It's not just poetic; it's biological. Your nervous system, shaped over millions of years living in forests, riversides, and wild places, still hungers for the living textures of the earth. A breeze across your skin, the scent of rain-soaked soil, the hush of trees breathing together – these don't just soothe you; they restore you.

Modern science is only beginning to catch up to what your body already knows. Trees release chemical compounds called terpenes, tiny messengers that you inhale unconsciously. Research shows they lower cortisol levels, boost immune function, and activate the parts of your brain that foster calm and creativity. As Clemens G. Arvay beautifully explains in his work, *The Biophilia Effect*[7], our relationship with nature is not metaphorical – it is a profound, biological dialogue between your body and the living world.

When you immerse yourself in nature, your brain shifts naturally toward states often sought through meditation: slower brainwaves, steadier heart rhythms, a dissolving of rigid

---

[7] *The Biophilia Effect*. A scientific and spiritual exploration of the healing bond between humans and nature. Sounds True.

self-consciousness. In the forest, by the ocean, even in a small patch of city green, you remember: you are not a machine racing against time. You are a living being, belonging deeply to a living world.

When you choose to be wild – to step outside and open yourself fully to this great unfolding – you awaken a part of yourself that still knows how to thrive, even when everything around you feels impossible.

Together these three 'adventures and investigations' are at their heart about the idea of letting go, letting go of unwanted distraction, of worrisome thoughts that capture us, letting sometimes go of our pain and discomfort. It is the non-judgemental tracking of experience as it unfolds in front of us, which gives us a tremendous perspective on what matters, what is important, helps us pay new attention to what is going on by maintaining a sense of distance in this case from ourselves. They are about creating the space between ourselves and the absorbing world, so that we can better understand what we can and cannot control, the chance to travel through the mindful gap, the mischief zone and the creative space.

And most of all let our bodies, mind and spirit rewild.

How wild are you?

- I have space in my life where I am by myself
- I am open to the moment and what it might bring
- I allow myself to be lost
- I saunter
- I have strategies for immersing myself in the here and now

Thoughts for me?

_____
_____
_____
_____
_____
_____
_____
_____
_____
_____
_____
_____

Chapter 11: Be Strong

Be grounded in the things that you are good at and love doing. Meet the world sure in your own worth, and respect only those who have earned it through their deeds. Build your life through practical intelligence. Keep an independence of mind.

Some of the time, I live on a rusty old narrowboat called Emeline near Cropredy. This is an amiable little village in Oxfordshire in England close to the River Cherwell, a relative of the Thames. The houses and cottages are often thatched and built of that uniquely warm, buttery Cotswold sandstone. Most of the time, nothing much happens as the Southern Oxfordshire Canal meanders and dallies on its way through, and locals loiter over warm English beer in the Brasenose and the Red Lion. In fact, not much had happened here since 1644 when Sir William Waller led the parliamentarians into battle against King Charles during the English Civil War and lost.

Apart from one day, every year. First, a camper van arrives spluttering a little through the village after a run down the M40. Then a Peugeot 307, then a Ford, and a variety of Toyotas; an old trusty, rusty Rover; a middle-aged couple on a tandem bicycle, grim lipped with effort, wearing Che Guevara T-shirts; then an embarrassed Mercedes, as coy as a large, well-engineered German car can be. Soon this trickle of motor locomotion becomes a flood as hundreds, then thousands, of cars arrive, in all states of repair, some pulling caravans, some with little-used tents strapped to the roof, crammed with bearded men, guitar cases, pewter mugs, bored head-phoned children gazing listlessly on England's verdant splendour, big-bosomed women in cheesecloth blouses with grey-blond hair pulled into a pony-tail; and everyone else from seventeen to seventy in jeans one size too small.

Every year, thousands of people gather in the fields outside the village, to sit in the sun, drink beer, eat a potpourri of global street food and listen to a folk-rock group who only had one particularly successful album, have never been fashionable and are now in their seventies.

The band is called Fairport Convention, and the bass player, Dave Pegg, is someone who was once very kind and supportive of two guys struggling to get somewhere with their music. One of them was me.

I am still in touch with Peggy, and a few years ago, we sat in his house in Banbury having a lunch of smoked salmon bagels and beers. We nattered about old times and the enduring popularity of Cropredy.

> 'We get full-grown adults coming along who were conceived in those fields,' he grinned.

He is very modest about the reasons for its continued success. When I asked how it had kept going for over twenty-five years, he explained:

> 'It's about camaraderie and the fact that you're with 20,000 like-minded people, having a peaceful time, some good beer, some good grub, and some good music. That's it, that's the gist of what it's all about.'

Too modest, I think. I do not want to be fanciful here, but those thousands do not just turn up to drink beer and make babies, or even to listen to the old songs one more time. Amongst the burger and vegetarian wraps, dreadful sunhats, and pink skin, something almost reverential is going on. Sure, it will be for lost youth and dreams of past times remembered, but also something more akin to acknowledgment, recognition, affirmation even. The band of grey-bearded men with shiny heads and battered guitars we recognise as having stayed true to something, stayed strong when others weakened. They kept playing.

I asked Peggy how, when so many other bands have disappeared.

> 'I've got my little niche in music as I suppose you do in any kind of job that you take on, you find what you're good at, in my case what I thought I was good at was accompanying singer-songwriters and playing bass and just being part of the rhythm section and trying to get the song to benefit while I played, not to deter from the song and to kind of add to it and to make it more interesting.'

> 'That's it, sometimes it works, sometimes it does not, but that's the kind of role of a bass player in this kind of traditional folk music. That was what I felt I was good at, and that's what I enjoy doing the most because I love songs, and I love to hear people singing songs, and I love backing guitar players. And that for me, is who and what I am.'

What stayed with me afterward was the simplicity of this as a life plan. Despite never being fashionable, considerable changes in the music industry, collapsing business models, it has delivered a forty-year plus career in music, hundreds of recordings, thousands of gigs, a million miles on the road. Achieved it appears by discovering what makes you feel strong and what gives you pleasure and always connecting back to it. Not a drive to be famous, not for adulation, but a simple desire to stay strong, to do what you feel strong at and what you feel called to do.

Being strong is about being rooted in the world and the realities that surround you, and being confident in your abilities, values, and beliefs. In other words, your strengths enable you to respond successfully to the reality you face. In psychological terms, this is sometimes known as self-efficacy, defined as your sense that you can have the ability to meet the challenges you face. Along with self-esteem, which is your regard for your worth, this is the heart of who you are.

Being strong changes your relationship with the world. It changes the relationship you have from one of dependence and supplicancy to one that is primarily based on equality: an interchange with the world based on your sense of self-worth and understanding. In this, you are much more grounded, seeing every crossing as a choice.

Being strong is developing that which you are good at and which you are passionate about. Being strong does not mean that you must be unbelievably brilliant at something. It is the things that you do, in the exercise of which you feel energized. Using your strengths feels simple, obvious, complete, whole. Through them, we discover ourselves, listening not to the judgement of others but the quiet clear voice of ourselves.

If the essence of who you are is your strengths, then being distorted or prevented from living through them, authentically and well, is not going to be right for you. Such a life would force you off balance, teetering somewhere on edge. Ungrounded, your head is in one place, your heart in another, and perhaps your body in yet one more.

It is difficult to see how you could be resourceful in such a place.

The question is how we free ourselves from the poison of negativity and limiting beliefs about ourselves.

The answer is by knowing and living in your strengths and renewing them. This puts you in touch with your genius. Genius is not about brilliant intelligence, but in the old meaning of the word, the spirit that guides you. (The same root as a genie and another echo of our cultural next-to worlds.) Genius also came to mean in Roman times the essence of something, its defining qualities, and talents. It is your genius that enables you to meet the possibilities that lie waiting for you in the borderlands and the weird worlds beyond.

Crafting a life in the tangible world

Like an artisan, we craft our lives from our strength hands-on with the raw materials we are using. This is the tangible world of our senses and experience. I think this is an often-overlooked aspect of Being Strong – connecting head and heart and our senses to the need for a tangible outcome. This is our evolutionary journey.

In the bookshop of the Smithsonian, that great institution in Washington, I bought, somewhat suspiciously, a book titled *How to Think like Leonardo Da Vinci – seven steps to genius every day*. In it, the author Michael J Gelb explores seven aspects of da Vinci's approach to life and offers a wide variety of exercises to develop some of the master's attributes in ourselves. One of them was to make minestrone soup very slowly and deliberately. I raised my eyebrows a little and wondered if the author was being facetious. But then I realised this was an exercise in engagement with the real world. Engagement through our senses.

To me, the most astonishing and exciting thing about Leonardo is his incredible practicality. He wanted to understand how the human body worked; how a man could fly; what was the quality of light; and how to defend a city under siege. And that curiosity was expressed and depended upon his engagement with the sensory actuality of the unfolding world – he was intensely connected to it.

We live in strange times when virtual abstract representations of the world have replaced our real experience. A world where apart from the twitching thumbs and the passive acceptance of image and sound, we are physically inert. Teenagers spend vast amounts of time in 'virtual' space; adults, particularly those in positions of authority, live in an abstract world of models, statistics, trends, and flow diagrams. People in power these days have, by and large, followed a path of academic study, University education, think tank, consultancy, and political office.

What seems to result is rational, abstract arguments and decisions which, although pleasing to a well-ordered mind, gain unfortunately little traction in the world. Far too often, this is the thinking of the 'They' in whom we are supposed to trust.

Abstract thinking means you can't picture an issue as it really is, or judge the situation and its impact completely; small, easily overlooked but important detail is often overlooked.

In my work, again and again I have seen the world represented as trends, flow diagrams, graphics and pie-charts. Most of the conversations that have been provoked as a result have been about what the data really means. As I have looked around the room, I have seen those present checking out, because they cannot connect what they are hearing and seeing to the experience they have.

There is a false dichotomy between intellectual work and practical work, the former being deemed more complicated and requiring higher intelligence. The truth is you think with your hands, your eyes, your ears, and a sense of smell and through physical movement. It is through these that we develop insights and practical knowledge of the materials with which we are dealing. Those materials are ingredients, processes, behaviours, or structures of our lives. You need hands-on experience of them to build your strengths to craft your world.

There is a massive resource of wellbeing and resourcefulness available to us when we connect the tangible to intellectual experience.

Without this connection to reality, we are forced to become mere consumers of the ideas and expectations of others without any understanding of how things work or of what they consist.

Adventures and Investigations

To become stronger in an Impossible World, it is a good idea at the start to disconnect yourself from any particular goals you have about the future. The argument through this book is to make yourself as strong and adaptable as possible and tying yourself too early to goals may mean you miss important features of your resourcefulness and potential. If being wild helps to see anew the potential in the world and in you, then being strong mobilises you to take advantage of this. You can set yourself some temporary goals when you have made this connection.

Sail the Seas of Serendipity and see what you discover

Play with things and ideas. Playing is about doing things for their own sake, because they are enjoyable. Consistent psychological research has shown this is the state when ideas come to you, when a-ha moments strike, where the future can reveal itself. Start with improving something you already enjoy doing or revisiting something you used to do. Then try something a little different that might intrigue you. Do something physical – that involves hand, or eye, or balance, or touch, or all of them. The chances are that, unless this is something you already do, you are waking up parts of your brain that have been a little dormant.

Learning a new craft or sport is immersive. You are likely to be engaging with all your senses. Research has shown this has a calming and anxiety-reducing effect. But more than that, you are re-engaging with essential sources of information and kinaesthetic, visual, tactile, auditory senses, all of which are massively liberating sources of memory and creativity.

In all of this, you are developing a sense of self-efficacy – the feeling of control and competence that you can get things done. You are grounding yourself in the spirit of mastery and control.

So **Be Strong** and:

- **Go work with your hands**
- **Go try Micromastery**
- **Go be a Polymath**

Go Work With Your Hands

He was an unusual bricklayer. He liked to have a cigar in his mouth, or one hand with a trowel in the other. He was a qualified member of the Amalgamated Union of Bricklayers. He was fond of home improvements and built himself a beautiful red brick wall around his vegetable plot and also a swimming pool and a goldfish pond. In his spare time was rather a good painter, other artists commenting upon his keen sense of light and colour. He raised pigs and wrote books, lots of them.

He was, of course, Sir Winston Churchill. He was one of many who can give the lie to the idea that to succeed, you must be ruthlessly focused upon one thing. All his life, he engaged in many different activities, many of them involving the skilful use of his hands.

Working with your hands, I believe, is a core activity that impacts a wide variety of different aspects of your life.

Most clearly and obviously, it makes us feel good. And feeling good or more specifically accomplished is at the heart of being strong. Kelly Lambert, a neuroscientist at the University of Richmond, says:

> 'When we move to engage in activities, we change the neurochemistry of our brains in ways that a drug can change the neurochemistry of our brain.'

As mentioned above, in modern times, we have tended to separate the intellectual and the manual, seeing the former as more critical and offering more prestige than the latter, which was seen as the preserve of the less intelligent and academically less gifted.

Increasingly, some people doubt this separation. Not only does working with your hands reduce stress and anxiety, but it also improves neuroplasticity – the ability of the brain to develop new neural pathways. Working with your hands puts you in touch with the environment, engaging with raw materials, seeing the world as something to be shaped and fashioned, and involving your creativity and inspiration.

Matthew Crawford was once an executive director of the think tank company in Washington DC and is now a part-time motorbike mechanic. He wrote the bestseller, *Shop Class as Soul Craft – An Enquiry into the Value of Work*, a *New York Times* bestseller.

A review of his book in the *New York Times* (5 June 2009) highlights the following:

> 'Unlike the electrician who knows his work is good when you flip a switch and the lights go on, the average knowledge worker is caught in a morass of evaluations, budget projections, and planning meetings. None of this bears the worker's stamp; none of it can be definitively evaluated, and the kind of mastery or excellence

> available to the forklift driver or mechanic is elusive. Rather than achieving self-mastery by confronting a 'hard discipline' like gardening or structural engineering or learning Russian, people are offered the fake autonomy of consumer choice, expressing their inner selves by sitting in front of a Harley-Davidson catalogue and deciding how to trick out their bikes.'

I must confess that, as a guy who studied philosophy and psychology at university, and has spent most of his life – at least in large part – working in the abstract world of consultancy and research, then the need to engage working with my hands has grown more and more apparent.

Of course, the music has always been there; playing an instrument leaves you no room to hide in terms of your proficiency, particularly when you are recording. But I also increasingly look to work with my hands to build my sense of efficacy, mastery, and, in the end, self-belief. On my treks, I have learned the peculiar sets of skills that keep me alive: looking after my feet, filtering water, hanging high bear lines from the trees, and navigation. I learned the hard way, the very hard way, the importance of packing a backpack well when you are walking tens of miles in unforgiving territory.

More recently, I have taken to baking, learning to make sourdough, focaccia, corn tortilla. I have discovered that dough is ready to bake when it feels ready. I have gathered berries in the hedgerows and made jams, jellies, and cordials!

What I experience in doing these things is not just the immense pleasure and feeling of accomplishment that they offer but so often how ideas and insights arise unbidden out of doing them. Ideas and insights which often wholly relate to some other, perhaps more esoteric challenge, I am facing.

Go try Micromastery

My old chum Robert Twigger[8], he of the story of a lost tribe of dwarves and adventures into the Sahara, came up with a quite brilliant idea of Micromastery.

Micromastery is when you make a challenge small enough that you can succeed at it to the highest level in the shortest amount of time. So, for instance, do not try and become a good cook, aim to become the world's best omelette maker. Do not set yourself to become great at drawings until you have spent some time learning to draw a perfect Zen circle.

In the preamble to his book *Micromastery* he argues:

> 'Whether it is making a perfect soufflé, painting a door, or lighting a fire, when we take the time to cultivate small areas of expertise, we change everything. We become more fearless learners, spot more creative opportunities, improve our brain health, and boost our

---

[8] *Micromastery: Learn Small, Learn Fast and Find the Hidden Path to Happiness*. Penguin Life, 2017.

wellbeing. We see knowledge itself completely differently.'

For me, we see it tangibly.

Go be a Polymath

In the triangle of England that is Birmingham, Lichfield and Derby, at the end of the 18th century, lived a group of friends whose extraordinary creativity and practical intelligence made, for a while, this spot, away from the elites and well-to-do's of London, one of the driving forces of change in the world.

Centred in Birmingham, they would meet once a month on the date that coincided with the full moon to ease the, probably inebriated, for some, journey home. They were led by Erasmus Darwin, grandfather of Charles, one the leading doctors of the time, a poet, garden maker, carriage designer and instigator of canal building. Other members included Josiah Wedgwood, who, from very humble beginnings as a potter in his brother's works, became probably the most significant industrialist of his age, more or less inventing modern marketing in terms of flagship stores, celebrity endorsements (Catherine the Great of Russia), streamlined supply chains, as well as continuing to research and develop new glazes and new products till the end of his life. He was also the social reformer with a humanitarian interest in housing and education. John Whitehurst was a poor clockmaker from Derby who developed radical a new mechanical apparatus, was one of the early pioneers of the science of geology and ended up a member of the Royal Society. Other members included Matthew Boulton, Joseph Priestley who discovered Oxygen and James Watt, the great engineer. They met to discuss and debate and share ideas around science, art, philosophy and politics. Several of them were pro-American independence and antislavery when it was certainly not fashionable to be so. In fact, there is evidence that Erasmus Darwin, despite his fame and being eminent enough to turn down the role of royal physician to King George, was the victim of a government sponsored smear campaign.

All this group seem astonishingly adept at many things, both intellectual and practical. For many of them with little formal education they excelled both in the dexterity of their hands and their brains. They were almost all definitively polymaths.

We see people like this as belonging to another age. The 20th century created the massive dominance of production line mentality, not just in the manufacture of goods but in the process of information. This, in turn, meant that people were required to become increasingly specialised, handling of a small bit of an ongoing process. But the whole of this approach depended upon the notion of a predictable world. Without predictability, it is impossible to see the world in such a well-ordered way. The world of borderlands, the weirdness the skills we need and the understanding required must be continually discovered. We all need to be 'lunartiks' now.

I know I am a good consultant partly because I learned the craft of dealing with a group of people as a folksinger. I hope that my years of travel being exposed to different perspectives of so many people have made me more insightful in working in a multicultural world. I know that any success I have had as an artist is due, in part, to the disciplined behaviours that working in business demands. I believe any creative problem-solving abilities I have in psychology or music or art or adventuring come from the same wellspring drawn from a lifetime of experience.

The remarkable people of history are nearly always polymaths. Hildegard of Bingen was a 12th-century German abbess who was a philosopher, theologian, composer, and poet. Some say that she was the pioneer of opera, sexology, and scientific natural history. Maya Angelou was an American author, actress, screenwriter, dancer, poet, and civil rights activist and possibly one of the most remarkable people of my lifetime. Did her time as a dancer inhabit her poetry – it sure did! Did her life skills as a newspaper editor, streetcar driver, and cook make her a unique academic – of course!

Our assumption often is these polymaths did all these things because they were and are super intelligent. The truth is probably the opposite – they excelled because of all the different things that they did.

Pursue things that interest you, excite you, and let them connect. You will find solutions to the challenges you have in places you are not looking for them.

The essence of who you are

Being strong changes our relationship with the world. Time and again, I have met people who are courteous, self-assured, and attentive. Not always, but very often, they were crafts people.

The impression is one of strength. The courteousness and attentiveness arise from a surety about who they are. It is not born of an overanxious need to please or to dominate. Such people have no need for approval beyond a sense of a job well done. Their self-assuredness makes them seem content as if they are marching through life at the pace which suits them and the things they care about. Through this sense of strength, their wholeself remains engaged.

Be Strong

- How might I do more with my hands?
- Where could I develop a micromastery?
- What am I interested in outside of my 'specialism' that I could pursue further and in greater depth?

Thoughts for me?

_____
_____
_____
_____
_____
_____
_____
_____
_____
_____
_____

Chapter 12: Be Experimental

Be curious, try things out without prejudging the outcome. Explore, adventure, take a chance, challenge your assumptions about yourself. Break a few rules.

When I was a young boy, I loved chemistry. My parents bought me a chemistry set and I happily followed the instructions to make crystals grow around pieces of string, do interesting things with copper sulphate and make strange, colourful smoke. The mischief maker in me couldn't resist making potassium permanganate crystals, small little purple things which crack loudly when you tread upon them. I got perverse pleasure from sprinkling them discreetly on the floor as my schoolfellows queued with their trays to collect lunch. My finest hour was to attempt to make the world's biggest stink bomb with a huge pile of candle wax shavings and a bag full of sulphur. I had the good sense not to try this at home but in a friend's house. My experimental career was temporarily put on hold following hysterical complaints from my friend's mother who had to go live with a neighbour for a week because of the smell.

At school I looked forward to the chemistry lessons in old laboratories of ink-stained wooden benches, high stools, Bunsen burners and test tubes, vacuum cupboards, and pipettes. I felt on the road to becoming a magician.

Each week we would do and write up an experiment. The write-up would always follow a strict formula. We would write a title, a description of the materials used and equipment, the methodology and the results, and a discussion. After a while I started to notice the title always began with the phrase 'an experiment to prove…' And I began to think that this wasn't really doing an experiment at all. It was more like following a recipe where you knew the answer before you started. Experiments I began to think were about finding out, exploring, being surprised.

There is the same trap in experimenting with your life. People try something new and when it is not immediately successful and they say out loud 'that proves I don't like it, I am not able, I don't want, it doesn't work et cetera, et cetera.'

This seems closer to being a lazy chef than a good scientist.

The results of good life experiments are more questions and choices. The questions are 'why did that happen, could I have done it a different way?', and the choices are 'what do I do with the learning I've just had and where could I go with it?'

The nature of experiments

This notion that experiments are about generating choices is fundamental to the idea of building resourcefulness. Every craftsperson I have ever met is constantly engaged in trying out new techniques, new materials, new ideas all arising from a need to be true to themselves.

So it should be with your life. Being experimental is important for two reasons:

(a) It is the best strategy for dealing with highly uncertain times when it's hard to grasp what works. It allows you to create options for yourself and set some goals, even though those will have to be continually reviewed and adjusted.

(b) It is a way of managing your own paradoxical nature. The insight offered by Michael Apter that we are constituted of opposing motivational needs means we have a life task to keep these in some sort of balance. For example, to feel you are achieving important goals and enjoying yourself *or* that you are fitting in and belonging and wanting to be free and independent. There is never a resolution to this conflict, as the circumstances in *which* you live your life continue to change.

For instance, how you balance your love and care for your family with your own needs to succeed and grow will need a constant reimagining of what works.

Experimentation is a formula for practical evolution – a way of keeping ourselves in constant motion. We rarely make one huge decision followed by a ruthlessly executed master plan. Experiments are a kind of conversation with the cosmos or at least the part of it in which you reside. A conversation in which both parties take part: you try something out, you get a response which can change what you think or how you behave and in doing so you change the cosmos, at least at a personal level, just a little.

Experiments develop neuroplasticity

The single most exciting development in psychology in my lifetime has been the growing insights into the neuroplasticity of the brain. This is the understanding of the physiological changes that occur in our brain as a result of our ongoing interaction with the world. It is a process that begins before we are born and continues till we die, enabling us to learn and adapt. In this respect, building itself new hardware, the brain is not like a computer. And its ability to do so, though it lessens between childhood and adulthood, does not disappear.

It is still in scientific terms early days in the process of exploring neuroplasticity but the consensus is rapidly growing that through activity both mental and physical you can 'rewire your brain' to overcome trauma, the effects of strokes, anxiety and depression. The idea of 'regeneration' is rapidly becoming more than metaphorical or hypothetical.

There are a number of different activities already identified as useful: from intermittent fasting to travelling; from learning a musical instrument to creating artwork; from non-dominant hand exercises to dancing. All of these increase the novelty and the richness of information your brain is experiencing. Experimenting with any or all of these will enhance your resourcefulness, and of course, help you identify new strengths.

Mindset to Be Experimental

What is the mindset of someone who can be experimental in their lives? Earlier in the book we talked about Carole Dweck's notion of a 'Growth Mindset' – the strong belief that your innate skills talents and abilities can with determination be improved. A 'growth mindset' is contrasted with a 'fixed mindset', in a nutshell two possible views of yourself that will profoundly determine the way you lead your life. If you take a fixed mindset then for you, strengths are cast at birth and basically unchangeable. You have to prove all the time you already have the strengths, skills, abilities to do what you need to do. Your challenge is to show, indeed, to prove this to others. It would be very hard to see how someone with a fixed mindset would enjoy being experimental when the outcomes are uncertain and may, in their own eyes, make them look foolish.

On the other hand, people with a growth mindset believe their basic strengths and qualities are things that are cultivated over the years through their own effort. They believe they can change, as can others. As already suggested in this book your true potential is unknown and unknowable and something you can keep exploring right to the end.

What is it that will give you this belief? First of all, you need to embrace your innate sense of exploration and curiosity, overcoming inhibitions which may reach far back into the shaping of your childhood.

Secondly, and related to this, you may need to develop a new relationship with failure. Fear of failure leads to inertia – it can be one of the ways in which you are taken hostage.

I've heard thousand times in my career 'I couldn't possibly do that, I would fail.' And therefore, he or she didn't try. But the point was never to prove you could or you couldn't, it was to discover and create choices.

In 2017, I attempted, with a companion, to walk the Benton MacKaye Trail, which stretches through Georgia into Tennessee over the Smokey Mountains, ending up in North Carolina. It is just over 300 miles, mostly through dense forest which clings to the sides of steepish mountains; the way is a constant succession of inclines which zigzag back and forward to make the ascent easier and valleys which slither down to little streams and rivers. The way was often hindered by 'blow downs', trees which had fallen across the path as a result of a succession of hurricanes that had passed through shortly before we arrived and whilst we were on the trail. And it was hot, really humid, such that my clothes remained damp always. We were what is called 'through hiking', carrying all that we needed: food, tents and other gear and collecting water from the muddy little creeks along the way. During the day we looked out for rattlesnakes and at night for black bears.

After 150 miles in I was done in! I was exhausted, totally dehydrated, my skin was sore and my feet blistered. But worst of all I was sick of the forest. At a tiny little settlement in the middle of nowhere my companion I separated and I stopped to recover, arranging to meet up again in a few days somehow. For the first time in my life, I had failed to complete the planned journey. I don't think I have ever felt so worthless.

In the forests we had now and then come across the graves of whole families who had attempted to carve a life for themselves out here in these wilderness borderlands. The borderlands, I thought, find you out.

I wrote later in my book *A Beautiful Broken Dream*:

> 'In the borderlands bullshit kills. You can chop a tree, build a cabin, cope with the heat, face the wolf and the loneliness or you can't. As simple as that.'

But in the months that followed I began to reassess that view. There is a huge component of feeling a failure which is constituted from our perceived judgement by others. It is often what the tribe thinks that really matters to us. And it is the judgement of the tribe that so often makes us afraid to try. Sure, when we experiment or undertake adventures, we will find often that we fail when we confront the reality of life in the borderlands. I know now that what matters to anyone who would flourish and grow is to embrace failure, to open up to it and let it do its worst. As I wrote at the time:

> 'To enter the borderlands and travel into the wilderness, whether that is the great forest, the burning desert, or the endless plain is not to brace yourself against failure but to embrace it.'

The fear of failure is a kind of captivity. You will be set free if you can disconnect the inevitability of failure from any sense of who you are and your self-worth.

Accepting failure is so much more than a learning experience, it is a proving experience as in a sharpening of our minds and skills and beliefs to better meet an uncertain world.

In a tennis tournament of 128 competitors, there are 127 failures and one winner. My great friend Stephen Venables, the mountaineer, once told me if you climbed every mountain expecting to get to the top every time, you would soon give up.

Adventures and Investigations

It is often a good idea to make a list of things that you have tried out and found you liked and were quite good at. Each of these represents a mini adventure where you have already succeeded. Things are made adventurous when you don't know totally what to expect; when there is a little bit of nervousness attached to undertaking them; when you feel you might get tested in some way. This combination of dealing with the unexpected, the feeling of personal stretch and the potential for discovery make up the potential for an experiment in many different ways. This could be trying something new and radical to see what happens. It could also be trying a familiar thing in a new way, such as the idea of using a non-dominant hand for familiar activities mentioned above.

Three suggestions for you to build upon:

- Go Explore
- Go Do Something You Really Wouldn't Usually Do
- Go Break Some Rules

Go Explore

What is it to Go Exploring? It isn't just the place. If you can get tour guides to take you up Everest and companies that can take you almost anywhere with a clear itinerary and a tight schedule, then exploring is not so much about where you go but how you get there. It's a subjective thing. Adventurous explorations are ambiguous: you don't know each night where you will stop; you can't guarantee to get to your destination; and perhaps you don't really know where your destination is! Perfect experiments with great seams of potential self-discovery.

A perfect example of Go Exploring is told by Sandy McKinnon in his book *The Unlikely Voyage of Jack de Crow*. An Australian teaching in an English public school, he decided to leave at the end of the summer term. Bidding adieu he left not in a car or taxi or train but in a rather decrepit Mirror dinghy. He intended to sail through English canals and rivers 'just to see where I got to – Gloucester near the mouth of the Severn, I thought'. But then one thing led to another and despite some rather dodgy map reading and planning and a variety of water borne misadventures, he ended up sailing around the English coast from London and across the Channel arriving a year later, having covered 4,900 kilometres, by the Black Sea in Romania. (A Mirror dinghy is totally open and just over three metres long!)

It's not that we should all attempt something as extreme as this, but the spirit of Jack de Crow captures something about Go Exploring as an adventurous experiment: it shouldn't be overplanned; it is about discovery and surprise not premeditated objectives; and we need to travel light, prepared to gather useful things on the way.

Go Do Something You Wouldn't Normally Do

I went dancing. Dancing brings out the shape shifter in us. It reduces strong men with loud voices to the outer regions of the wedding party, lurking, foot-shuffling and eye-avoiding until enough alcohol is consumed; turns the dumpy little girl into a swan; or makes a blonde sylph of loveliness career around like a carthorse on casters.

For me, dancing was an experiment, something to explore rather than an area where I needed to prove myself. Although it did suggest one thing. I dance like a bear. An enthusiastic bear sometimes. A bear with a sense of the beat. A bear with a certain *je ne sais quoi*. But a bear none the less. Knew I would, Ursus Major genes.

So why did I dance on that hot afternoon in a studio in Prague with Michaela and her friend Leon? It was because it seemed something outside of me, something I only dimly understood. People who dance well occupy a different space to other people. You can see it in every move and line; the floor does not rise up to meet them causing them to stumble nor does it fall away causing them to sway. Nor do those who dance well gaze into the eyes of another like they are holding onto an axe murderer. Most of all they do not look like they are reciting their thirteen times table in their heads whilst simultaneously recalling the assembly instructions for a particularly fiendish piece of flat pack furniture.

What did I discover? I saw aspects of who I might be that I had not really considered before. Michaela and Leon have a physical intelligence I can only grasp at. Michaela as a dancer is an actor: she can move, in a quarter beat, from the smouldering aristocratic line of a Spanish flamenco dancer, to the giggling effervescence of the Cuban girl on the street corner who looks sexy and knows it. Leon was smooth, explosive, riffing on the subtleties of rhythm and space. I was not so present: perspiring, demented and blundering: for those who remember him, like a slightly hysterical Ted Heath. I realized one huge difference between us was that I was desperately trying to get the salsa, the samba *right*, not make a mistake, whereas Michaela and Leon flirted with the rules, trying to get them, in a particular way, *different*. They were bending the rules, creating new variations, teasing conventions. It gave me the choice to think about myself physically in a different way. Until that point being fit had been about having stamina and losing weight. Since then, I have striven to see rules as a kind of friction to spark creativity and exploration (see below).

And it made me think how we get stuck sometimes being self-conscious when we need to be self-aware. As I trotted back and forward, carefully stopping to waggle a buttock on the fourth beat of the bar, an incredulous voice in my ear couldn't help but whisper, 'Just what do you think you are doing, Rhino-feet!'

Self-consciousness is paying too much attention to our shaped-social self, how it looks and will look to others. Self-awareness is a different thing altogether: it is to be completely absorbed in the moment, in a kind of dialogue with it where the edges of where you stop and the rest begins become blurred. It is like making love: best done with a focus on the matter in hand. Self-consciousness tends to get in the way.

Overall self-consciousness is a self-imposed limitation whilst self-awareness is a door to liberation.

Go Break the Rules

One way to start to move on from the tyranny of self-consciousness and experiment more effectively is to realise how arbitrary so many of the things are that we feel we couldn't or shouldn't do. There is a rather wonderful book by Taras Grescoe called *The Devil's Picnic*[9]. It recounts a year he spent travelling the world consuming food and drink banned in various countries. This included: Marks and Spencer's poppyseed crackers and chewing gum in Singapore; Epoisse

---

[9] *The Devil's Picnic*. MacMillan, 2014

French cheese in New York; absinthe in Switzerland; and a long search in Spain to consume threatened-with-a-European-ban bulls' testicles.

As we have seen, from the beginning of organised society, those with the power to shape what is deemed acceptable have actively sought to keep the rest of us in check. In fact, what is often addressed to us in terms of what is good for *us* is just a wind up. Some days I think the most insidious and elusive control is the social value that regards dependability and predictability as positive, and changeability and unpredictability as necessarily negative and anti-social.

Experimenting by breaking the rules is at the heart of creativity and creating choice.

A great example of this need for orthodoxy and rebellion is the story of the painter Manet. In the middle of the 19th century, he started to paint in a way that upset the conventions of socially acceptable 'good art'. In his pictures, real women stare back at you from boldly painted canvases of apparently crude brushstrokes, whereas his more conservative contemporaries executed with microscopic attention to detail, enraptured and rather portly nymphs floating on clouds above an Arcadian temple. In places Manet appears to have missed bits and it seems patches of canvas poke through. For several years he was scorned by the conservative elite of Paris, his paintings actively prohibited by civilised opinion from being hung on the walls of the Salons. But then people grew tired of the old tasteful art and looked for something more vibrant and challenging and as Manet shaped and influenced other painters with similar sensibilities, he ended up being the leader of the new conservative orthodoxy. Art, like our tribes and ourselves, evolves on the axis of stability and change.

There are so many possibilities for you to rebel! For a start you can rebel against yourself. Make a long list of the things you don't like and don't do and start doing them. Remember this list is at least in part one given to you through your interaction with others, captured in the stories you tell about yourself. Remember for the most part it is arbitrary, selective and fictional!

One of my challenges in this respect was oysters. I spent several decades of my life certain they were a kind of chilled, salty snot. Eventually the mystery of why such a thing could produce the look of near orgasmic reverence on the face of my companion proved irresistible. A whole world of seafood textures, tastes and challenges were thereby opened up.

This may be a trivial example, but it does highlight the difference between experiments to prove and experiments to explore mentioned earlier. So many people put the metaphorical oyster in their mouths, screw up their face, shaking their heads with certainty that their lifelong assumption has been confirmed. You need to confront the 'oyster' not with a fixed mindset but with the growth mindset of learning and discovery. Perhaps following an old psychotherapeutic technique, start by acting 'as-if' you liked it already. Think 'is this the best oyster I have ever eaten?' Which of course it will be!

Maybe it's me, but it seems there are so many rules to break. Pointless rules which have nothing to do with anything more than something, 'they' have decided is proper and good. Ignorance can be bliss. I am a songwriter of limited technical understanding. My good friend and creative colleague, Christopher Lydon, with his first-class degree from a major music school and career as a composer and arranger, laughs at the fact that there is scarcely a single piece of music I have ever written that doesn't contravene some 'musical rule'. Being somewhat an anarchist himself, he delights in helping me bring these aberrations to the world.

You can find so much about yourself by asking the simple question 'Why?' 'Why do I believe this? Why do I always…?'

Of course, there are rules which rightly we should not break and rules which we choose not to. We do not need to be pointlessly disruptive any more than we need to be thoughtlessly compliant.

An 'experimental life' is an endless source of discovery, fun and accomplishment. It is the way we grow and a way out of which a new direction a relationship with the world can emerge.

Don't be afraid

As Helen Keller said: 'Security is mostly a superstition. It does not exist in nature, nor do the children of men as a whole experience it. Avoiding danger is no safer in the long run than outright exposure. Life is either a daring adventure or nothing.'

Be Experimental

- Make a list of all the things you don't like doing. Which are you going to try first?
- Design yourself a DIY expedition. Where could you travel if you did not know where you would stop each night?
- What is the one thing which you are certain that can't do? Prove yourself wrong.

Thoughts for me?

_____
_____
_____
_____
_____
_____
_____
_____
_____
_____
_____
_____
_____

Travel with companions

Chapter 13: Travel With Companions

Make sure you venture into the borderlands of life with people who are committed to you, who will be prepared to sacrifice for you and you for them. People who will tell you the truth and fight for you when you are not there.

I was on a trek from the top of the Atlas Mountains out in the desert. With a Berber friend, Moha, and a couple of muleteers and their mules, we were crossing the Anti-Atlas Mountains.

With us was a dog. The dog was a handsome, more-or-less retriever, a bit fly-infested but with a golden coat. The Berbers mysteriously, therefore, had named him Black. He belonged to none of us. Not to me, not to Moha, and not to the muleteers, Mohammed and Hussain. He had simply joined us a few days back, up in the High Atlas Mountains, across the intervening desert between there and the Anti-Atlas range we had spent all day climbing. Generally, Berbers like cats and dislike dogs, but Black had struck up a bit of a relationship with Moha, and we all made sure Black had something to drink and some scraps to eat.

It was late and getting dark as we pitched our tents, and I watched the others struggling with the big poles and creaking canvas of their tent, as it was tossed about in a particularly fierce and gusting wind. I saw no point in wasting time with the flimsy thing I had been given, which was made of the second cousin to Chinese paper. The rain seemed to be the last thing to expect up here, and I decided to sleep outside under the night sky, something which I did for the rest of the trip. I created a sort of open sarcophagus with bags around my sleeping mat to keep the worst of the dust off. This particular night, I was feeling unable to eat, so I lay down to sleep. Black came over to inspect me, tilting his head to one side, quizzically, as if thinking, 'So you are not allowed inside either?'

I patted his head, and he turned his big brown eyes towards me and stared into mine.

> 'We are both a long way from home,' he seemed to be thinking.
>
> 'Home is where the heart is,' I said aloud, remembering an old lyric.

I couldn't help believing Black understood. He lifted a paw slightly and then turned and not far away circled round in the grit and dust and settled down to sleep, and I did the same. I looked for my old iPod, intending to stare at the stars and listen to some music to ease into slumber, as I lay in my open tomb. There was no sound except some snoring from the tent next to me and the gentle stiff flap of the old canvas in the wind.

Just at the threshold of sleep, I was startled by Black suddenly scrambling to his feet and barking once very loudly and menacingly and then continuing to growl in a low, ominous way. There was an answering challenge from the darkness, and a call-and-response of threat and counter-threat ensued as a pack of wild dogs prowled around in the gloom. I think they were initially attracted to this remote place by the deserted camp a little distance away. In the twilight and darkness, they circled our little refuge.

Black sat bolt upright 'on guard,' and I settled in my sleeping bag, bush knife at my side, and tried to remember Ben McNutt's instructions on killing coyotes. Every so often, Black, presumably deciding the pack were getting too close, would charge off into the darkness, and there would be a sharp bark, even a yelp. He would calmly reappear sitting upright while checking things were under control before lying down again and slipping into watchful sleep. Reassured, I put on my iPod headphones and listened to Dark Side of the Moon, the sad old dude that I am. Black was the best of companions.

Everyone is lonely

You may be feeling now that the central argument of this book is that we should move away from the tribe, which shaped our upbringing.

But this is not completely true: moving away is to psychologically free yourself from the servant and tribal mindset by which the tribe determines what you think and believe. It is to recognise that how you 'fit in' is a choice you alone make. That does not mean you somehow abandon the best that the tribe offers.

As I have said before, life is not one thing or another, it is one thing and another. The perspectives and the choices that give us independence of mind and action, and also the sense of deep affiliation and mutuality that is at the heart of making us resourceful enough to flourish in the borderlands of the weird, strange world that awaits us.

But it is the oddest thing – with everything from the size of our underwear to the probable date of our death out there to be known by the curious and mildly insane – with no barriers to access, we are lonely. When we chat with friends we have known all our lives via the internet, we are more available than we could ever have been. And yet many of us feel disconnected. We live in communities where our neighbours are often strangers to us, in towns that are not where we were born.

So, what have we lost?

A sense of belonging.

Of being born into a tribe.

Is this why one of the most popular websites is about helping people trace their ancestors?

Why is conversation so reassuring?

Evolutionary psychologists such as Robin Dunbar have argued that language itself is less about functional problem solving and more about building communities through the chatter and gossip. This enables a sense of cohesion and identity to develop. Dunbar argues that it was the 'connecting/reassuring function of language that enabled human groups to evolve to 150 person tribes from the much smaller groupings of other primates which are held together by *physical* grooming, a much more time-consuming activity. It is a rather beautiful thing to think of, that for the vast majority of us, online and offline chatter is the metaphorical search for bugs, twigs, and mucky skin that reassures and enables us all.

As we saw earlier, the world is becoming an increasingly lonely place. And the consequences of this loneliness as we seek to build our ability to cope with an Impossible World is frightening.

If the reality of tribal and small, intimately connected communities disappeared in the blink of an evolutionary eye, then the need to belong to one has not. And perhaps our current obsession with social media, such as Facebook and Instagram, is simply a reflection of a deep need within us to connect and share; to share opinions, feelings, objects, thoughts with people who affirm our world view. And this is when it gets dangerous. Socially we search for people 'like us', people who can bring a sense of security and identity in a world that is threatening and in which we can feel anonymous and overlooked. We band together through social media, and the advertisers and the political manipulators lick their lips and feed on our fears.

Think about the messages you receive about the world you are in now from people you know and feel connected to. Are they complex and diverse, or is there a strange consolidation in which you are always reassured that the group you are most wary of are indeed mad? But these are not relationships; they are temporary hostels of prejudice. No one challenges in these, there is only a reinforcement of prejudice.

I wonder if one of the qualities experienced by people who live in more traditional communities is that a more abundant array of relationships is available. Sometimes it seems in the age of the 'nuclear and disintegrating family', relationships with relatives are more distant, less involving, same-sex friendship groups are weaker, more superficial, and we have lost a sense of interdependency. The people who can tell us the necessary things we *don't* want to hear! The people who can challenge us to think differently!

The word that describes this best for me is 'companionship.' The root of the word comes from the Latin *com* meaning *with* and *panis* meaning *bread;* simply those we share bread with, with all the mutuality and trust that implies. And yet it seems to me, highlighted by our compulsive search of the wireless desert, we live increasingly in societies in which companionship is under pressure. Is it because we have been disconnected from our tribal nature? And through this, the way we relate to others seems to have shifted from a deep awareness of the collective whole to something brittle and transient?

Companions, I realised long ago, are part of the warp and weft of almost every culture and celebrated in its stories and tales, from the *Band of Brothers*, *Secrets of the Ya-Ya Sisterhood*, to *Snow White and the Seven Dwarfs*. In all of them is woven a cloak which can keep out the bitterest blast and shade us from the most relentless glare. Every guru from Jesus and Buddha to Freud and Elvis was sustained and enabled by the love and friendship of those around them. Though they must face a defining moment on their own, it is through their friends and companions they have been sustained and nurtured for this moment.

And every Don Quixote has a Sancho Panza

And so it is with us, to grow and flourish the conversations and attention from others in whom we feel we have trust, rapport, and a sense of shared identity. Instinctively, we understand the basic human need to be heard. If we are not heard, we do not feel whole. But it is more than that; it is through conversations that most times we think and decide. It is in the ebb and flow of the dialogue of the common man and woman that ideas are born and nurtured; that dreams are shaped into reality; that a wild notion becomes a life-changing opportunity. And I believe this has always been the way, since the beginning, since the first non-verbal moment when we looked at each other and recognised our common cause. It is what helped to make the 'Lunartiks' the astonishing group of friends that they were.

One of the great joys of my life as a psychologist is that the things, I have always believed instinctively about people are increasingly shown to be valid and important through the gathering wave of research evidence now becoming available. Evidence that is murdering the myth of the self-interested, self-obsessed man exploiting and manipulating those around him and revealing that fact it is kind, open, trusting groups that outperform others in terms of productivity, innovation, and other measures of success. While at the same time being mentally healthier places to work. A study by Nicholas Christakis, Professor at Yale University amongst many others, concluded:

> 'Humans everywhere are pre-wired to make a particular kind of society, one full of love, friendship, cooperation, and learning.'

And they do this not because it is seen as some morally righteous way of existing but because it is effective. It works.

Humankind by Rutger Bregman is a bestseller that challenges the traditional mean-spirited view of human beings with a brilliant overview of the mounting evidence that undermines this. In it, he tackles what he calls the 'veneer theory' of human nature: that that our niceness, our amiability, and our respect for others is but a thin coat easily torn under any pressure to reveal a nasty ravenous mind.

If 'Being Wild' implies intimacy with the animate and inanimate environment, a deep rapport with the rock, the soil, the scudding cloud, the bird on the branch of the tree, then we also have within us the need and ability to be intimately connected with other people. This is not just the physical intimacy of lovers or a parent and a child, but an emotional and spiritual identification with another. It is a surprisingly practical quality of being human.

It is like performing music together

Playing around the clubs with my old chum Tim, we would have a repertoire of over a hundred songs and tunes. Rarely did we ever bother with a 'setlist' or running order, or if we did, we would soon ignore it. You see, we just knew what to play next based upon an inarticulate but powerful sense of where we were and where the audience was. Often, we did not tell each other – or the audience – what we would play next, we just started: on time, together. Sometimes halfway through a tune, Tim would change rhythm or tempo, and I would just know. All of this was a rough and crude version of what any half-decent jazz band can do. Or any great football team. Or a theatre company. Or family. It is how the Bushmen hunt, how they survive in an extreme and challenging environment.

Without this collective inner harmony, it seems to me that groups of people can only at best function in a self-conscious, somewhat forced, and rather clunky way. Which I suspect is how many of us do, much of the time.

Intimacy goes way beyond 'belonging'; it is tapping into the essence of who we are, and maybe that is why it can become a rare and vulnerable thing. But it is the well-spring from which companionship draws life. What hurts one of us hurts all of us. And this seems a natural, not learned thing. Neuroscientists have proposed the existence of 'mirror neurons' in the brain that 'fire' when something is observed happening to someone else. So, we see someone bang his or her head and say 'ouch' or one gets too close to the fire, and we wince. And the closer we are to the person we are observing, the stronger the effect is. This reaction is unconsciously prompted.

So, from the bushmen tracking, in the first light of dawn, the Oryx, the Kudu, and the Porcupine through the millennia, this intimate shared consciousness has woven people together, has continued to shape who we are: collaborative, connected, concerned. A large part of us is inherently collaborative, as more and more research in evolutionary psychology seems to reveal This collaboration provides us with a set of social behaviours which can easily be overlooked in the picture of the individual free agent, acting only out of self-interest. We sometimes underestimate our capacity for self-sacrifice, working for the greater good, and the pure love of working with our fellows.

Collaboration is a clear and present feature of Confucian thinking but is also a powerful if less celebrated feature of western behaviour. All this must be rooted in our ancestry: in the stalking of the game, and the irrigation of the fields we have evolved to look after each other. Without it, we could not have survived.

This is a fantastic ability, through which we can build on the wisdom of others. And in such conversations, we, without awareness, tap into the wisdom and insight of our ancestors. The freedom to evolve, to renew ourselves, or even to survive may be a hard one, even an impossible one unless we travel with companions.

The question is, who do we identify with and feel we belong to? Or would it be better to say, who should we focus on belonging *with*? As my friend Nick Owen told me when we discussed this, many of our friends do not wish to come with us on our journey. We can love and respect them for this, but we must not let them tie us to living in the past. We can keep and cherish them but also seek companions who can help us evolve.

I have been lucky in my life with some of my friends. Yes, there is rapport, that incredible, instinctive understanding between people who are not kith or kin but whose lives have become enmeshed through shared stories and a kind of sublime chemistry. Yes, there is rapport, but there is also synergy. The best companions are distinguished by significant differences and who, arising from these differences, are not afraid to confront, clash, and conflict with another. Those I cherish do not seek to control me but to challenge my path so that I evolve well. This is a tough love that is distinguished by its rarity and its bravery. It is a special friend who will risk the regard of another for their love for them.

The best of companions is not wholly like us; they may only travel with us part of the way, they may be on parallel journeys themselves, and we should give them the space to do so. I have been in the desert with companions, and I have been in the desert with accidental fellow travellers. With the former, I emerged encouraged and renewed; with the latter, I merely survived.

Adventures and Investigations

I remember years ago working with a group of people who had enjoyed great success together over a lengthy period and built real friendships and understanding. And then the company they worked for announced a restructure and reorganisation. Members of this team were going to lose their jobs. Some, as the result of the sell-off of an operation, would be working for another organisation. And then others would remain. There was a massive sense of loss and hurt. And there was anger aimed at me. Not that I worked for this organisation but here I was trying to create working relationships that encouraged problem-solving and decision-making in the most effective way possible.

> 'Don't you feel ridiculous,' I was asked, 'preaching about open relationships and on the level of communication when this has happened!'

> 'Perhaps I do,' I said. 'But you have more power here than you think.'

I was looked at with suspicion and disbelief.

> 'In the end, I am here to help you work together effectively whatever.' I paused and then asked, 'So who owns this group'?

There was silence. Then someone said, bitterly:

> 'They do.'

> 'Do they?'

Again, silence and then someone offered.

> 'Perhaps we do?'

> 'Exactly!' I said. 'You – and nobody else! – owns every single relationship in this room. It is past, present and future, in your hands, and no one else can touch it. What happens next is yours alone to decide, and I know no means by which anyone can stop you!'

Many years later, many of that group are still in contact and supporting each other.

I think the idea of having a network, and of how important it is, is now well understood. Things like LinkedIn have systematised how we manage them and build them. But Travelling with Companions requires much more than the functional, I-scratch-your-back-if-you-scratch-mine nature of some people's understanding of these relationships. Sure, in this world, a good list of contacts is helpful, but here we are talking about people who will sacrifice for you and you for them. It seems we might have hundreds of people in a network but only a few can we be so invested in that we call them companions.

- **Go Open**
- **Go Connect**
- **Go Collaborate**

Go Open

From today tell the truth always.

In a world of manipulation, distortion, dissembling and plain lying, power will flow to the truth sayer. People are drawn to the truth sayer. They are authentic and worthy of trust. We honour them even though we may not agree with them.

People who are open are trusted are listened to and heard. They are told the truth in return.

If you are a truth sayer you will find you stand on stronger ground. You have freed yourself from the negativity of the false and avoiding.

I have often said that one of the odd side effects being a psychologist is you are sensitised to untruth, you hear lies.

Many, many times working with teams all over the world I hear those in the room avoiding the truth, not saying what they think, saying instead what people expect to hear. Maybe this is because of the hidden conflicts that flow around the room or the autocratic, even bullying style of the leader but always the energy is low, the discussions aimless and the decisions vague. And then somewhere sometime, hopefully with a little bit of my help, the truth sayer speaks up and the atmosphere changes. Energy flows, people can feel nervous and relieved at the same time; things move forward and others join in. The leader, if he or she has any sense, responds to this positively and meaningfully. I have been there when the leader has failed this moment of truth and the energy, the productivity collapses but the truth sayer goes on being regarded as powerful.

The liar may have friends amused and entertained by the insincere and the preposterous, but they have no companions, for they are untrustworthy.

One of the hardest lessons of my entire life is to have learned to say the truth *always*. It is not the case that I think I have ever particularly told lies, but I know that I have avoided the truth. Often, I have done it for good reasons. Because I didn't want to cause conflict. Because I did not want to hurt someone. Because I wasn't sure of the value of it. But the end the result was always wrong. It undermined who I was.

Now I try to follow the way of the great Socrates and make sure that what I say passes three tests: is it true, is it kind and is it necessary? It is this last one that can be hard to judge. The test is, I guess, do I feel it benefits the other person or persons in some way? And remember another great voice from classical times, Marcus Tullius Cicero:

> 'If we are not ashamed to think it, we should not be ashamed to say it.'

Start today, in the mirror: tell yourself the truth. Not a list of inadequacies but a celebration of what you believe about yourself and the world. And make a point each day to tell someone what you think, what you believe, what you hope.

Go Connect

When I was 16, I was in a rock band, just a hustling, rough bunch of teenage overenthusiasm. Other mates were in other bands. One of those friends was Kev. He was better than most of us. At first, he played drums and was really, really good. And then, inspired by the great Phil Lynott of Thin Lizzy, he became an equally fine bass player. In those days you could measure the life expectancy of a rock group at the bottom of the heap – like us – in weeks, and Kev and I would find ourselves playing together in the various incarnations and reincarnations that suddenly appeared and – equally suddenly – disappeared. And then Kev was gone. He moved out the area and went to live up north playing in increasingly professional and successful line-ups. He joined Christie, whose most famous song 'Yellow River' meant that for 20 or more years he toured the world. He played with Graham Oliver's Saxon and recorded with everyone. Including – now – me.

Out of the blue, unexpectedly through social media and more than 35 years later, we were back in contact with each other. He came to see a gig I was playing in my hometown and was very positive about a new song I had just written.

'It would sound great with a really good bass part,' he said, and a few weeks later flew over to Cong in Ireland where I was making an album and delivered on his promise with an unbelievably strong sinuous bass part that he had worked out in his head on the flight over.

And a few years later we are still writing and recording together. Along with Chris we have played dozens of gigs and festivals, toured Germany and launched a successful podcast.

The thing is that Kev made the effort to connect. Someone always must reach out. You will know people in your life who you once had rapport with, but time and circumstance has moved you on. These days with social media, it is easy to reconnect. It is not guaranteed that these re-connections lead to new companions but the return if they do could be enormous.

And then there is the opportunity to connect with new people who may be fellow travellers. I came to a point in my life a few years ago when my music and my writing would be jostling for position at the heart of what I was doing. I had good companions and true but none of them knew much anything about this world. Therefore, there was no-one for me who would understand its peculiar challenges and could share advice and feedback. I made a deliberate effort to connect with people with whom I thought there might be some rapport, writing to them to explain what I was doing and what I was trying to explore. Most often I did not get a reply. One who did was Jason Webster, author of a book I really admired called *Duende*. I met him in Spain for a very boozy seven-hour lunch in one of Hemingway's old haunts. He was generous with his stories and thoughts and advice. And he put me in touch with Robert Twigger, another writer with whom, as I have mentioned, I have shared many adventures. If I were going to congratulate myself on this, it would not be for the ambition of writing to Jason but the willingness to pay the cheap Ryanair fare to fly to Valencia!

The lesson is: if you want to travel with companions see it as something worth investing in.

Go Collaborate

People get confused about collaboration. Often, they confuse it with cooperation. Cooperation is something different altogether. Cooperation happens when I volunteer or agree to help you with your plans. Collaboration is when people work faced with up challenge they see as mutual think together, decide together and act together. Each contributes his or her own unique set of strengths.

If we are facing an impossible time and need to move through the borderlands towards the weird world, we may need new way of working together. I imagine the companions that we travel with as a group of comic book heroes, each with a special magic power which can be available to the whole group at the last moment of crisis to save them and win the day. This gift of diversity is so often ignored. If we bunker down in this turbulent world with people just like us, we may rue the day that someone who does not like us is sitting in another bunker.

Collaborating with people enables the richest understanding of what is really going on, generates the greatest number of insights and options on what to do about it and makes sure that, following this, everyone knows how to help.

Work in the future is going to be more like the making of movies than the idea of working in fixed roles in ongoing companies. You know how when you see the start of the film there is a mind-numbing ten minutes in which all the companies who 'made' the film are highlighted. There is no one particular arching organisation, just a network of operations that have come together to make this one production. Each of them has brought something special to the opportunity and helped shape the result.

This has always been the model with which I have worked, whether that is in consultancy, music or even writing. The best team possible, each with their special magic powers, are assembled for that project. This has never worked where the people involved are not 'travelling companions'. Where there has been no trust, mutual understanding, or rapport then there have been difficulties.

To be able to mobilise the people who get you can help you and go the extra mile may save your life!

Consciously thinking about growing companionable relationships through the different activities you engage in may be the best insurance policy you have ever invested in.

Travel With Companions

Draw a map of your social world. At the centre put yourself. Mark important others in your life in terms of their closeness to you as companions (they will tell you the truth, they will challenge you, they will support you, they will be a sounding board). The less close you will put furthest away. If the relationship is strong and ongoing, connect that person to yourself with a solid line. If the relationship needs some work on because over time you haven't invested then make it a dotted line. Make time to repair.

Think of what these close-to companions can offer you. *Is* there something missing? Does this create a support gap? Are there people who are further away from you who might become companions?

Thoughts for me?

_____
_____
_____
_____
_____
_____
_____

Chapter 14: Take the First Step

With self-compassion and craftsmanship, start your journey. Take the first step away from the village, your servant-mindset, and begin your liberation.

Atlas Mountains, 2017.

> 'We should go back,' Moha said, 'it is too technical.'
>
> 'How long will it take to go the other way?' I asked.
>
> 'Oh, about three to four hours.' My heart sank. It was day one and I was already feeling weary. I really hated the idea of retracing steps.
>
> 'How technical?'

'Very.'

'Show me,' I said.

We clambered to the edge of the ridge. Some distance below us, maybe 75 metres, I could see a steep path around the side of the mountain levelling out somewhat after a while, to take a zigzag route down towards a flatter expanse of grass and bush. To get to the route though there was a series of short, maybe three metre, vertical climbs to a narrow ledge, followed by another and then several more.

I considered my options carefully. I was tired and had some chance of falling off. In England, the descent would have involved ropes and helmets and things. And apart from some sessions on a climbing wall I am not a climber. On the other hand, walking back along the ridge and the scrambling down a long scree slope and then a three to four hour walk to a point I could see below me seemed a poor choice. Not for the first time in my life I weighed up the distance between potential extinction and feeling more knackered and found it much narrower than might be expected. (I once decided it would be better to die in the snow on the Mer de Glace on the slopes of Mont Blanc than struggle any more in waist-deep soft snow to the exit via a bubble lift some distance away.)

The call to adventure

That is it, isn't it? You start to understand how you might change, to better understand how you might survive and thrive in this Impossible World. You see strengths in yourself which you are excited to explore. You have experimented with things and see the choices you have, and your companions now look at you and say, 'it's time.'

And you hesitate. You hesitate to live your life in the way that you want it.

That little first step suddenly looks like a yawning chasm.

Like the diver on the edge of the high board looking down at the extent of the plunge he is about to take, pausing for a few seconds, minutes, hours, weeks, months, years. A lifetime. Or he, and we, slink away, frustrated even angry with ourselves. 'Next time,' we promise ourselves. 'Next time.'

You know, as Joseph Campbell put it: *'If a person has a sense of the call but remains in the society because it is safe and secure, then life dries up.'*

What has happened? What has got to happen to take that step, the step into the borderlands and a new relationship with your world? Why do we totter on the tipping point and how do we let go of the past and embrace the future?

It was interesting when I asked some of my friends what the issue around taking the first step was. Those who, it could be argued, had already set off out into the borderlands, as writers, entrepreneurs and explorers were simple and brutal about this hesitation, calling it a 'laziness' or a 'lack of perspective', or wrote handy tips on how to get over it. For others, the question was more troubling, as if asking it was in itself vaguely threatening: 'uncomfortable'. It was something you ended up 'turning 360 degrees around.'

Perhaps part of taking the first step is to really understand what is happening. You should perhaps not be surprised that you might hesitate, for in this moment of truth you are about to cross the threshold into a new world. You are leaving the assumptions of the tribe village in which you have grown. A fresh story or a new way of looking or being in the world is about to take over your life which others may not understand.

You can feel the stakes are high. You can sense the potential for catastrophe. This first step is a step into the unknown in which you instinctively realise you cannot control all the outcomes. You can easily be captured by sense of competing commitments. You might feel you are heading towards something you may enjoy much more than life now, but you are surrendering some security. You might feel the future offers a chance to be free and be an individual, but you will lose the warmth and affection of the people who will remain in the old world. For example, taking a job overseas and leaving your old friends.

And your wonderful paradoxical nature with all those oppositional motivations that Mike Apter describes means you can feel you don't really know what you want; that how you see yourself and your relationship with the world is elusive. It is as if you cannot pin down who you are.

The result: you can easily procrastinate, putting off today what you will not get around to doing tomorrow.

But do not write yourself off yet. Procrastination at any time over anything that should be done large or small is not a character flaw or a lack of your ability but an evolutionary created bias to prioritise short term needs over longer-term ones, however much you may cognitively feel those longer-term ones are important. In evolutionary terms not being in the here and now is more likely to get you eaten. The result is now that any short-term anxieties in taking the first step overcome any feelings about future benefit of taking it.

Dr Hal Hershfield, quoted in the *New York Times*, has shown that at a neural level we perceive our 'futureselves' more like strangers than parts of ourselves. 'When we procrastinate, parts of our brains actually think that the tasks we're putting off – and the accompanying negative feelings that await us on the other side – are somebody else's problem!'

It is a 'no-win' challenge if we are not careful. Putting off the first step may alleviate very short-term anxiety about taking it but almost immediately leads to feelings of self-frustration, feelings of lower self-esteem and negativity. Ongoing progress procrastination can be very destructive to mental and physical health, leading to low life satisfaction, depression, anxiety, and poor health behaviours. It is very hard to break, because in the immediate present putting off the change rewards you with an immediate sense of relief.

And of course, the more significant and therefore threatening we see this first step, the greater the reward for not doing it! The idea that our 'futureself' is not our own is a hard-wired idea in our brain which has important implications for adapting to life in the borderlands.

Adventures and Investigations

How might you take the first step? The first four rules of the road support you. When you are on the solid ground of your strengths; when you are wild enough to see the possibility around you; when you are willing to experiment with who you are; and when you have true soulmates. Make sure the first step is towards a motivationally rich and purposeful future. Test your vision for yourself against your 'wholeself' purpose from Chapter 4. Is it going to deliver? If it looks like it is, then it will.

And then:

- Go Now
- Go Let Go
- Go Prepared

Go Now

And then perhaps the solution is that proposed by 'Brahim, another Berber friend, as we trudged up a very steep incline. Take shorter steps but do not stop.

Take the step you can manage, remember the physics; stride length times height can quickly make the effort exhausting. Take the step towards what you intuitively know is the right direction. Do not get involved in battles in your head between the voice of the tribe and the voice of freedom. Remember you are not taking one huge leap from the Village to the Weird World, you are taking the first step! Take a smaller step. Do not imagine the first step is the whole journey. Do not deny yourself the pleasure of the journey of getting there by imagining it can be done in one bound. Enjoy the feeling of momentum building and a new story taking shape. A new story which as you sit in the late evening by a crackling fire, as a cold wind rattles and mutters outside the door, as the clock ticks towards midnight, you are proud to tell.

Go Let Go

Treat yourself with compassion. Self-compassion is a psychological state in which we are kind to ourselves and understanding of our failures, indeed that we treat failure very much as the positive step towards something better we explored in Be Experimental. Self-compassion might be the rare and fine oil that lubricates your resourcefulness. It has been shown to increase your sense of self-worth, your levels of motivation and encourage emotions like optimism, wisdom, and curiosity.

Self-compassion is about letting go. Or acceptance. Acceptance that things will go wrong, things will not be easy all the time, that people will let you down. If you take that first step thinking otherwise, then you are foolish. What you must not do is waste your energy in negativity on feeling angry with yourself or others or disappointed or humiliated. Self-compassion says 'these things happen; I am no less valuable because they did. I will go on.' It is also about accepting that ultimately you have no control over the choices of others. One of the hardest lessons in my life was for me to acknowledge in the end that the only choices I can truly take in the world are for myself.

Self-compassion looks for the positive and the affirming – it does not deny weakness or failure, but allows learning to happen and someone move on.

Go Prepared

Sometimes I think I see changing yourself as a bit like pushing at the most enormous stone cartwheel. You push with all your might, but it almost feels like it is pushing back. Here the laws of momentum apply. The huge effort at the start to get even the smallest movement is repaid as the wheel starts to turn and its own mass starts to pull it forward. The resistance, as we have seen, is made up of your uncertainty, fear of failure, and the imagined disregard of onlookers. To get that wheel to turn we might think of the challenge in terms of what I have called the performance cycle. You do not just, unless we are a little crazy, walk to the end of the high board and dive off.

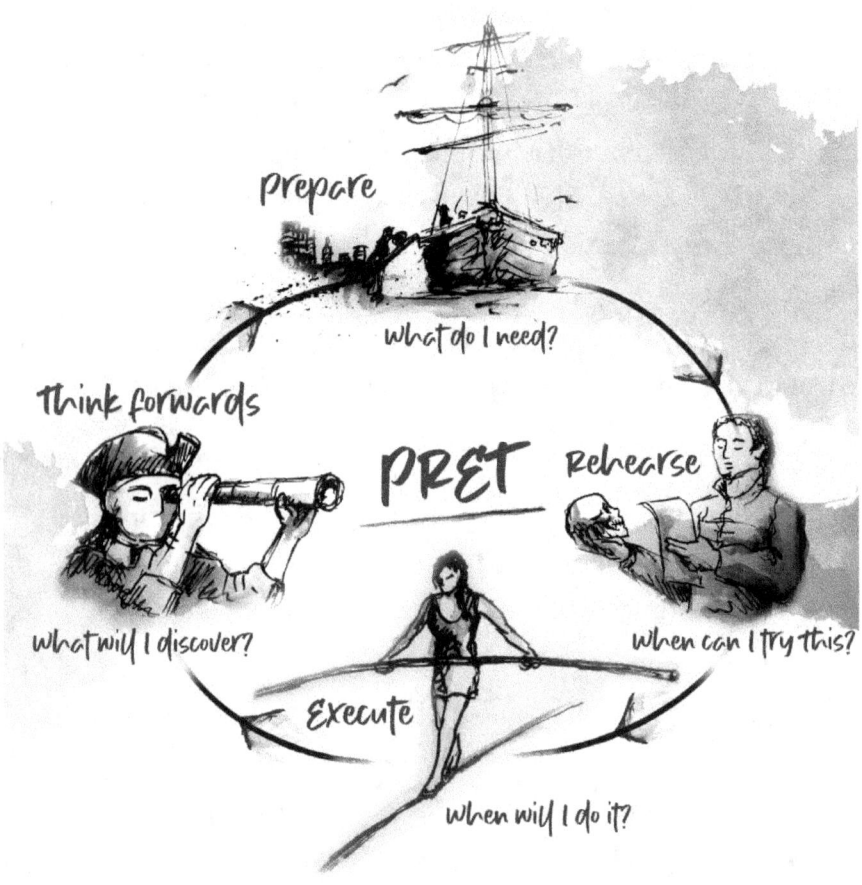

You *prepare, rehearse, execute, and think forward* about what you have leaned and might do differently next time.

Preparation means exploring the challenge you face and bringing the other rules of the road to bear upon it. Be wild asks what is really going on here, which different perspectives do you need to take up the challenge? Be strong asks what strengths will you need to rely upon – which do you have which do you need to develop? Do not be afraid to be experimental in how you tackle this challenge: there may be different ways of meeting it, one of which will suit you better. Who are the companions that will help you meet this challenge and what do they know about it now? This preparation builds confidence and self-reliance, but it is usually a mistake to jump straight to action.

If that first step is to count you might need to rehearse it first. Preparing for something and doing it for real use quite different parts of the brain. Preparation requires analysis and problem solving when the action can easily be stopped and readjusted. Rehearsal is something where real actions flow in real-time with complex demands being made cognitively, emotionally, and often physically at the same time. For example, I could teach you all the separate chords for a particular song, one at a time, until you knew them all. But unless you are an accomplished guitarist and played a similar sequence of chords before each time you change chord in the song you are likely to stumble, hesitate or indeed stop. This is true for physical activity; but it is also true of psychological activity, as in thinking of things in new ways. The in between stage which is so often missed out is rehearsal. Rehearsal gives us flow in real-time. It enables us to keep going; even if we make a mistake, we can correct it. We prefer to see Shakespeare, unless we have a very weird sense of humour, when it has been rehearsed. We rather hope the surgeon when we are lying there on the operating table has rehearsed before what they are going to do. Yet in so many things in life we move from preparation to action in one go; and sometimes, we do not even bother about the preparation.

Evolution has given our brains a wonderful technique for enabling on the spot rehearsal. It is called visualisation. We can mentally rehearse conversations, actions, behaviours in the most deep and meaningful way. Research has shown that mental rehearsal of complex activity enables proprioception: the exact muscles and nerves which will be involved in future activity are engaged in a kind of ephemeral way when we visualise, enabling new neural pathways to be engaged and consolidated.

Rehearsal preparation means that we gain the momentum to execute an idea to take that first step. And as we step out into the psychological borderlands for the first time, we keep engaged with what is happening and what we are learning; for whatever we anticipate, the reality will be in some ways different. This thinking forward enables us to discover the new 'rules' that allow us to flourish in a new world.

You are now ready.

Over the Edge

Over the years through my adventures, I have been the witness to or even a participant in activities in which someone takes a critical step, one they have shied away from perhaps on several occasions. It might be an abseil, tipping over a cliff on a length of rope and walking down at right angles to the rock face. It might be performing to a small audience a song you have learned. It might be finally saying what you really think in a business meeting.

In every case, in taking that step people are almost in a daze afterwards, say they feel changed, that from now on things will look differently to them. They have been, at least for a moment, wholehearted. They have liberated the wholeself within. Some of the greatest joy I have taken from my work has been to feel I have been a little catalyst in such moments.

Climbing Down

And back to that dilemma in the Atlas Mountains at the start of this chapter. With Berber nimbleness, Moha climbed down first to each ledge, often facing outwards into the void.

I felt dubious.

But then again, I had prepared and rehearsed for this moment. Over the previous months of the winter, I had been trying get fit. I had walked regularly with my old chum Tim up in the

Derbyshire Peaks where I lived, I had done my 10,000 steps every day for my Fitbit; but I knew that wasn't enough. The thought of 20 miles plus a day through a remote and rugged region of deserts and mountains was enough of a prompt to send me twice a week to a climbing wall inside a church in Derby. I was not anticipating I would be climbing any difficult faces, but I did want to increase my sure-footedness, core stability and ease of travel.

The good people there found me an instructor called Rob who was a slight and spry guy who was training to be a stuntman. He would arrive at the sessions having just injured himself fire-eating, fencing, or crashing cars.

On the first day, he watched me climb up a route.

I got to the top quite quickly and felt rather proud of myself.

> 'You climb like a typical bloke,' he said contemptuously, 'thinking you're just gonna haul yourself up with your arms because you can! Climbing is problem solving and physics. Come down here.'

And with references to those well-known mountaineers Pythagoras, Euclid, and Sir Isaac Newton, he introduced me to the idea of using my own weight as an aid not an obstacle to my ascent. I had to climb up walls using only my legs for upward propulsion, I wasn't allowed to raise my arms much above shoulder height, I had to try on occasions to get myself horizonal to the ground about three metres above it. For days after I would walk around like a saddle-sore cowboy muttering to myself:

> 'Bruising occurs when one forgets that to every action there is an equal and opposite reaction…'

And so I followed Moha.

To tell the truth, apart from one heart-in-my-mouth moment when the rock I was clinging came away and bounced past Moha's head, I enjoyed it. The trips to the climbing wall with all the preparation, rehearsal, execution and thinking forward had paid off.

When we got to the sloping path. Moha looked at me with a note of approval.

> 'Ha!' I thought, 'I may be the fat bloke with the dodgy knee, but don't underestimate me!'

Take the First Step

What is the small step you can do now, this moment, to change something important in your life?

Map a change for yourself on the Performance Cycle below. You have just taken the first step!

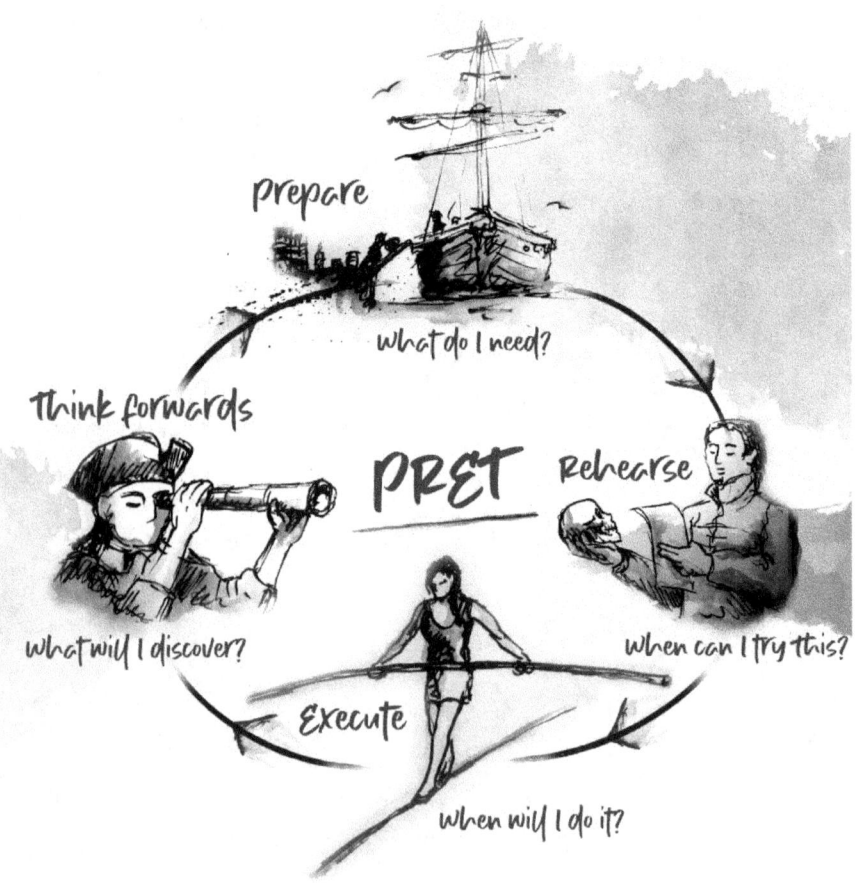

Thoughts for me?

Thanks

This book was written during the COVID-19 lockdowns and marks an important moment for me, when the two strands of my life – 'psychologist and leadership consultant' and 'musician and adventurer' – finally, and completely, merged into one.

The time this merger has taken is, in part, a product of the evolution of business culture in the last twenty years. Back then, even having a beard was enough of a provocation in some places!

It is also due, in part, to me developing the confidence to see that all that I do feeds insight and knowledge into everything else, and that diversity of experience is at the heart of understanding and practical action.

Notwithstanding this reconciliation of my separate journeys, this book would not have happened now, and in this way, without the enthusiasm, encouragement, and support of Orla Flynn, who has always brought her wholeself to her life and the wisdom thereby gained to this project.

I must thank, too, my daughter Lucy-Jane – a natural editor and wise critic – for her comments on early chapters, which helped me refine my approach and clarify my thinking.

My gratitude should also go to Dewayne Ashton, who produced on demand great illustrations based on my vague ideas and scrappy sketches, and to Mal MacKenzie for the cover design[10].

Thanks go to my old friend Peter Harvey for his editing. Incredibly quick, happy to be pedantic only when it matters, accurate and learned – he is a perfect foil for my erratic prose.

I must acknowledge the help of my long-suffering brother, Mike, who, once again, rescued things from the mire when needed!

Many of the ideas in this book have been developed with the wise counsel and critique of Marie Shelton, and have been tested on the organisations and individuals who worked with us for many, many years at Apter Development LLP.

---

[10] Cover design of the first edition.

To Chris and Kev, compadres both in the mad game of life.

Finally, to you good people who bought this book before it was published, your confidence and generosity meant a lot to me.

Steve Bonham
Church Broughton, Derbyshire, England
September 2020

About the author

Steve Carter / Steve Bonham

Steve is a singer-songwriter and folk musician with a deep love for Americana and a gift for storytelling. A seasoned performer, he has appeared at clubs and festivals across the UK and the United States for many years. He has released multiple solo albums and is a proud member of the legendary band The Long Road. His music – often rooted in place, memory, and identity – has earned hundreds of thousands of streams. Among his notable works are evocative songs inspired by his off-grid treks through forgotten places, off the tourist trail.

In addition to his musical work, Steve is an accomplished writer for the stage. His musical 'How to Survive and Thrive in an Impossible World – with a piano!' enjoyed a successful three-week run at the Edinburgh Festival Fringe and is appearing this year at Brighton Fringe. He often performs alongside his long-time creative partner, pianist, arranger, and producer Chris 'The Bishop' Lydon.

Steve is also a published author, with several books to his name. These include *A Beautiful Broken Dream*, which chronicles his journey through the southern United States, and *Stumbling Over Eden*, detailing an ambitious walk from the peaks of Morocco's High Atlas Mountains to the edge of the Sahara Desert. In 2024, he released his children's book *The Spirit Dog*, accompanied by a tour of schools and libraries across England, supported by Arts Council England.

Outside of the arts, Steve is an award-winning psychologist who has worked across the globe – in Asia, the Middle East, Europe, North America, and South America – focusing on leadership and team performance, conflict resolution, and wellbeing. He is also a sought-after speaker at conferences, festivals, and public events, bringing insight, humour, and humanity to everything he does.

stevebonham.net

Photograph by Colin McMahon

Other books by the author

Available from artisan-creative.com

Stumbling Over Eden

Starting with the simple but quite crazy idea to walk from the top of the Atlas Mountains into the Sahara Desert a distance of 540km, this is a tale of companionship, exploration, self-discovery, and freedom. It is also about the beautiful almost mystical resonance that occurs when you submerge yourself into a landscape. This tale involves the search for a lost tribe of dwarves, discovering the lair of old warlords and an almost mythical Krupp cannon, travelling with a spirit dog, and finding Eden. It is a book for anyone with an adventurous heart.

> 'A boy's own – and girls! – adventure of a trek, from the High Atlas Mountains, across the Anti Atlas, then following the exotic river Draa into the Sahara. You will fall into a world and people as fascinating and friendly as any fairy tale.'
> - Mike McHugo

A Beautiful Broken Dream

A 'trail book' of a journey mostly on foot through the great forests of the southern states of the US and then a trip along music road, from Ashville to Nashville and New Orleans Endeavouring to avoid irritable bears, rattlesnakes, agitated natives, over-exuberant creeks, and a whole variety of other challenges, this is a journey into the heart of Appalachia and the Southern States and the music that flows from it. What emerges is a wry, funny, provocative, and highly personal view of this land and the 'truth' it holds for all of us.

A Little Nostalgia For Freedom

Steve Bonham invites everyone to consider again their own responses to some of life's big challenges: why many of us never quite do what we what we mean to do; why, when so often we are comfortable, do we feel restless; how do we respond to sheer paradox of existence and flourish!

'Perhaps the ultimate question of life is 'when do we fit in, and when do we fall out?"

In doing this as he takes on us on a journey through the pirate towns of Morocco, the Atlas Mountains, to London, Hong Kong, and the Sahara in search of the source of and the resolution to this, our Little Nostalgia for Freedom.

The Spirit Dog

Written by Steve Bonham.
Illustrated by Tasia Graham.

A heartwarming and true story about a mysterious dog named Black who adopts author Steve Bonham and his friend Moha as they journey through the High Atlas Mountains towards the Sahara Desert. Through the heat, rocky mountains and deep valleys, encountering deserted kasbahs, streams of salt water, remote villages, a young snake, and packs of wild dogs, this is an enchanting and haunting tale of adventure and companionship.

> 'A touching true story about friendship, love and how one dog united a group of travellers on a perilous adventure through the Atlas Mountains. A fantastic read.'
> - Maisie, aged nine

More at **thespiritdog.life**

About Artisan Creative

Celebrating the extraordinary stories of ordinary folk.

We believe in the 'artisan values' of craft, inspiration, authenticity, and the love of the raw materials.

Artisan Creative was created to provide a platform for developing distinctive books, recordings, and performances.

> We have performances and workshops available based on various themes and ideas, including *How to Survive and Thrive in an Impossible World – with a piano!*, *Stumbling Over Eden* and *The Spirit Dog*.
>
> We've toured performances, workshops and shows across the country, in theatres, arts centres, community settings, libraries, schools, colleges and rural venues.
>
> Perhaps you have a venue or community setting that we could bring our unique performances to?
>
> Find out more at **artisan-creative.com**

www.ingramcontent.com/pod-product-compliance
Lightning Source LLC
Chambersburg PA
CBHW071234070526
44583CB00017B/2181